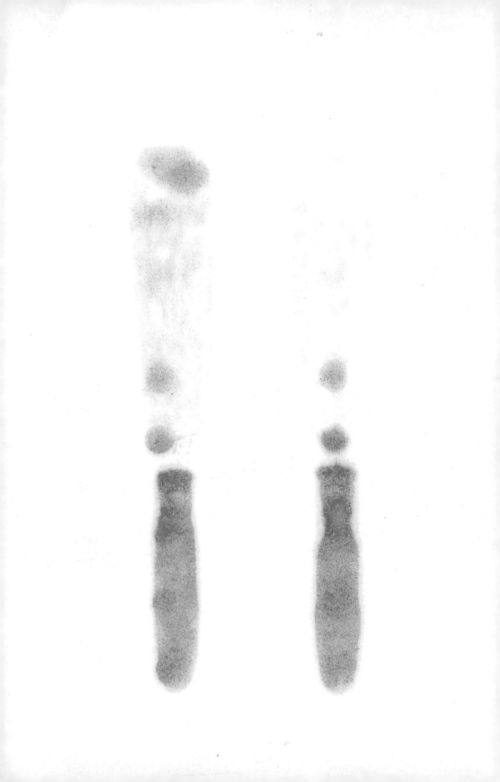

SCHMOCK-SCHMOCK!

Books by Steve Allen

SCHMOCK-SCHMOCK!

by *Steve Allen*

With Commentary By Thomas Ellis Katen

Doubleday & Company, Inc., Garden City, New York, 1975

Library of Congress Cataloging in Publication Data

Allen, Steve, 1921.
  Schmock-schmock!

  I. Title.
PS3501.L5553S3   818'.5'407
ISBN 0-385-09664-X
Library of Congress Catalog Card Number 74-12672

To David

STEVERINO AND THE MOCK OF SCHMOCK: STEVE ALLEN'S CONTRIBUTION TO AMERICAN HUMOR

By Thomas Ellis Katen

It was the night of January 16, 1974, anno Domini, a night that belonged to a great funnyman. For a quarter of a century Steve Allen had not only filled empty nights, late and early, with his sparkling wit, but had also brought integrity and honor to the world of television. Now he was being recognized for this achievement on a Wide World of Entertainment special: "Hi-Ho, Steverino." Steverino's comic pals, of course, honored him by saying all of the dishonorable things they could imagine. Finally the moment of Allen's comic revenge arrived. He started by observing, "I knew I was going to get a chance to nail you guys tonight, so I've been keeping a file on you. It's a nail file!"

"That's my kind of joke," he added. Not only is the joke his type—the funny thing is that the *remark* is his kind of joke. For it is in the wry reflection on the world and all in it, including his own material, that we see a kind of humor at which Allen is an accomplished master.

It is not easy to categorize the humor of Steve Allen because it wears many faces, all very funny. He is not above low comedy or slapstick, but neither is he beneath highly sophisticated wit. He can be a most intelligent punster or an uninhibited clown. Allen's bag of comedy tricks includes farce, parody, physical schtick, satire, philosophical witticisms and nonsense. The being of Steve Allen is a beautiful reconciliation of opposites: One moment he may be as serious as Karl Marx, the next as zany as Groucho Marx.

In the film *Coconuts* Groucho informs Chico that a viaduct leads to the mainland. Puzzled, Chico asks, "Why a duck?" After all, "Why a no-chicken?" Groucho explains that the water is deep and if Chico tries to cross over a chicken he will understand *viaduct*. But Chico still doesn't understand. Groucho tries again. If Chico went horseback riding and wanted to ford a stream he couldn't, because it's too deep. That's why there must be a viaduct. Chico wonders why you should want a Ford when you gotta a horse, and, besides, he still can't understand why a duck. The Marx brothers were masters at the art of horsing around with words, and in doing so, on a deeper level, revealed the barren quality of much verbal communication. Steve Allen also is tuned in to the absurdity of verbal communication and knows how to turn us on to it. On a radio program a guest mentions the Simi Valley. Allen comments: "You folks back East may not realize that we have seamy valleys out here. In fact, we have some of the seamiest valleys you've ever seen."

Steve Allen not only makes us laugh at the ridiculous, but often makes us think. A musketeer is defined as a soldier with a musket. We all watch The Three Musketeers in action, but how many have noticed that they are rarely observed carrying muskets? It takes Steve Allen, so tuned in to language, to observe that.

With his sensitivity for the ridiculous a clever comedian can make us think about the ambiguity of words. Groucho Marx remarked, "One morning I shot an elephant in my pajamas. How he *got* in my pajamas I'll never know!" The zany comic antenna of Steve Allen is similarly sensitive to ambiguity. One night on his Talk Show Allen was in the audience when a woman inquired, "What do I have to do to sit down in front?" Steve's immediate response, "See a chiropractor."

A perceptive funnyman such as Allen not only makes us think while laughing, but can make us think about the *way* we think. People often connect ideas by psychological associations rather than logic, and that can leave things logically disconnected. By ridiculous exaggeration Allen reveals how absurd a "psychological" chain of reasoning can become. On his TV show a pretty "Miss Prune" recommends *Prune Whip*. Steverino comments, "A man would have to be pretty low to whip a prune. Think of it, my friends; a prune is little, it's old, wrinkled, defenseless. You show me a man who would whip a prune, and I'll show you a man who would beat an egg."

Behind the ridiculous that is so often on the tongue of Steverino is a most logical and fast-working mind. Interviewing actor Michael York, Merv Griffin detected an aristocratic note in his voice, and said, "From the way you speak and your accent, Michael, I would suspect the upper class." Allen interjected, "Merv, you've always been suspicious of the upper class." Steve further observed, "That's how the proletariat are these days."

Many comedians would like to stop the world so they could get off with their old jokes and routines; Allen's humor is usually moving with a velocity greater than the world's. The type of spontaneous, imaginative and creative comedy he introduced in the fifties was far ahead of its time. Allen has such a feel for what is happening here and *now*, he can take the squarest fairy tale and render it in hippiest version. See his *Bop Fables* account of "Little Hip Riding Hood."

Hugh Walpole observed life is a tragedy for those who feel and a comedy for those who think. Life is a beautiful comedy for Steve Allen, certainly a man who thinks about fundamental issues such as war and peace, crime and punishment, freedom and slavery, wealth and poverty. His intellectual orientation is in evidence even when he is being funny. In the course of his mocking, Steve Allen gets in a share of muckraking. In 1971, when some in the media quaked from the verbal lashings of Spiro Agnew, Californians were shaken by an earthquake. Allen was informed that in response to the earthquake President Nixon was dispatching

Spiro Agnew. Steve's ad-lib response: "We go from one disaster to another."

On another occasion Mort Sahl remarked, "When Ronald Reagan was running for office, lo these many years . . ." Steve answered, "Low is the right word."

As if to give validity to Steve's witty remark, when Randolph Hearst had food given to the poor as a ransom payment, Reagan reportedly let the thought slip that it might be well if the poor got botulism from the food. At a hospital dedication a few days later Allen wryly noted the institution would include a Ronald Reagan wing, a special facility for the treatment of botulism.

In the fearful fifties, when it was widely believed we had to restrict freedom of thought in order to prevent the "Commies" from taking over and restricting freedom of thought, the national mood was such that thought-provoking political humor was not considered a joking matter. Yet even in those days before Watergate, Allen fearlessly led his humor off limits into such areas as "corruption in high places." On his Sunday night NBC-TV show Steve directed his humor at concrete specifics of high-level political scandal and also got some general advice across. In a man-in-the-street interview a man was asked if he would accept costly gifts if he were a public official. He answered, "That would depend on what the gift cost." Allen explained, "It will cost you the next election."

Official corruption is not the only target of Allen's political wit. He also directs his barbs against political insanity left and right. On the TV show "That Was the Week That Was," which no longer is, Allen, with an assist from Buck Henry, did a classic job of ridiculing the already ridiculous extreme Right. As Mr. Robert Wretch, Allen explained himself as founder of "several prominent hate groups." Psychiatry is a plot by Commies, communism is a plot by the Jews, and Judaism is a plot by the psychiatrists. Further, a Minuteman leader was forgiven for being a child molester because he only molested left-wing children. This outstanding political satire can be read in Steve's *Bigger Than a Breadbox*.

Allen also has some witty words for feminist extremists, who themselves seem obsessed with words. When one Women's Lib group criticized the practice of naming hurricanes after women, Steve doubted it would sound better to call a tropical storm "Irving."

Steve's humor raises questions about religion as well as politics. One night on "The Tonight Show" he was discussing the subject with guest host Joey Bishop. Referring to a passage in the New Testament, Allen said, "Jesus was looking for a fig." Then he added, "One would wonder why he didn't *know* where it was, considering all he had going for him."

Steve is capable of irreverence toward those who are even greater than the gods, the powers that be in the television networks and government bureaucracies. In April 1956, the Academy Awards' show had just ended and Steverino's "Tonight" program was just beginning. Steve would also bestow some awards. One was for art, given to the man who conceived the best design of the year, and there on NBC network television there appeared, large as life, the well-known CBS insignia. Now that's irreverence!

It has been known for sometime that the drug D.E.S., fed to cattle to make them heavier, is a cancer-producing agent. When the Federal Drug Administration finally got around to banning the dangerous substance, it allowed it to remain on the market for an additional five months. While the public was still eating meat infested with D.E.S., Steve's wit was biting F.D.A. His caustic comment: "So, you folks who get cancer during the next five months . . . no hard feelings."

Mark Twain observed that nothing can stand against the assault of laughter. Steve Allen is proficient at the art of assaulting with laughter. On his twenty-fifth anniversary TV Special, Allen, noting that his friend Tim Conway "usually plays a bumbling, inept dumbbell," asked, "And why not?" Conway was so dumb, Allen said, he thought *The Exorcist* was the life story of Jack LaLanne.

On the same show Allen said, "Some people say all the really

xiii

great comedians are Jewish. Rowan and Martin, you have certainly proved that tonight."

On his talk show Merv Griffin asked Steve if he ever saw any "pornies." Steve confessed that once at UCLA, as part of discussion material, he saw two minutes of a pornographic film. "And," said Steve, "Merv, you never looked better."

While the Allen wit can be piercing, it is never poisonous. The very way Steve makes fun of others is such that you *know* he is not hurting them but having fun with them. Once a skeptical Yiddish cobbler shocked people by going to synagogue on a religious holiday. The rabbi wondered why he came and said to him, "I thought you didn't believe in God." The cobbler responded, "I don't, but how do I know I'm right?" There truly was a tolerant man. The beautiful thing about Steve Allen's humor is that it is so tolerant and human. Even when he is putting someone down it is done with such sensitivity you feel he is saying, "But how do I know I am right?" When Allen insults there is always his human laugh that tells us he is not laughing at the person but with him.

Those who insult with malice aforethought are out to get someone. There is no one Allen is more out to get than himself. Steve performed for a cops-and-pop show at the Hollywood Bowl. It began with a demonstration by twenty-four police motorcyclists and an appearance of two trained police dogs. Steve said, "While waiting backstage I was bitten by a dog and run over by a motorcycle."

On the TV roast of Allen, Tim Conway said Bob Hope once called Steve the Adlai Stevenson of show business, but Tim said he is more the Henny Youngman of politics. That joke, that really roasted Steve, was written by Allen himself. Not only can he give it; he can take it. Critic John Bailey maintains Allen is funniest when something is *happening* to him. And do things ever happen to him! Once he was flown around Los Angeles while standing on the wing of a World War I airplane. On another occasion he had to dive through a ring of fire. He has even done a circus high-wire act. Before going up Steve was informed the net would break his fall. What he wasn't told until he was on the rigging was that if he didn't fall correctly the net could break his neck. He has actually been attacked by tarantulas, overrun by large red ants, been in a box blown up by dynamite, driven sixty miles an hour into a solid block of ice, and walked into a screened cage full of bees.

A girl friend once asked me how someone as essentially serious as Allen "could be so crazy." Why does one who has a great deal of wisdom play the fool so effectively? Why not? Allen has impressive company. In the Bible, in Shakespeare and Dostoevski it is often the fool who turns out most wise. By accepting the role of victim, the fool, the clown, attains the wisdom of learning to take it and thus better adapts to the vicissitudes of existence.

Throughout history the Jews were persecuted and oppressed, and yet are still standing. An important dimension of their strength was a rich sense of humor and a capacity to laugh at themselves. While mighty and aggressive powers vanished from history, the Jews survived. What is more, for three thousand years they survived without a country. Considering his comic role as victim it is interesting that on his anniversary TV Special Steve Allen seemed surprised that he had survived professionally for twenty-five years. Twenty-five years on TV, of course, is like three thousand in the arena of history. Certainly during that period many mighty talents have vanished from the tube. Saturday, March 24, 1973, Steve Allen performed a comedy concert to a packed house at Carnegie Hall; before the show even began he was greeted with a lengthy standing ovation. Allen has not simply survived—he has triumphed!

It was the view of French philosopher Henri Bergson that we laugh at that which is too methodical and inelastic. The great comedians can show us how to be more elastic and get with the flow of life. Human elasticity and spirit of life are qualities inherent in wild screwball humor. A Steve Allen can open our eyes to such a world of madness.

In this overmechanized world people have become so tightly wound up they are taut with tension and on the verge of breaking down. The funnyman, who behaves in a delightfully silly manner, helps unwind us. He who clowns is in revolt against enslavement to the tyranny of mechanical efficiency. When Steve Allen wants to know what a "clyde" is, or when he lays such neologisms on us as "fern" and "kreel," when he lets go with a wild falsetto "schmock-schmock," he liberates us from the monotony of rote response.

Never mind definitions. When Steverino gives out with a "schmock-schmock" he is doing what is unexpected, getting us out of those narrow ruts of routine. This is a way of *mocking* overseriousness and rigidity. A dull guest on Steve's TV show lamented, "I seem to be bogging down." Steve told him, "You can't bog down, you haven't bogged up yet." A funny way of saying, "Don't be tense, get with it."

We may think of the "schmock-schmock" factor as the mocking capacity. Instead of being ruled by impersonal forces, those who understand the secret of the schmock-schmock factor know how to make fun of life and thereby can rule themselves. People who are up-tight might find it easier facing life if they could give a little schmock-schmock here and there. Oddly, not even many comedians possess this uninhibited factor. They can perform standard routines, but you can't imagine them sounding off with the cry of the wild bird.

There are words, apart from any meaning, that are funny in themselves. This is true of many Yiddish expressions. Schmock-schmock is a sound that also has intrinsic comic significance. In the sound itself there is conveyed a sense of the absurd that lets us understand reality need not be so boring as we sometimes make it. Steve Allen possesses the schmock-schmock factor; his style of comedy mocks all that is boring.

Allen reports that ever since he was a child he devoted himself to "horsing around," having a good time, saying funny things, making ridiculous faces. Steve began to perfect this talent on a professional level when he did a radio program in the 1940s. On this show such characters as "Manuel Labor" and "Claude Horribly" were developed. Ever since, Allen has been blessing us with the gift of laughter through his zany improvisational humor, his "madlibs," his uproarious questions in response to answers (The Question Man—Father of Carnac), his bopping around with fairy tales, the madness of his angry readings of actual "Letters to the Editor," his "Funny Phone Calls," his knack for interviewing crackpots, his hilarious and spontaneous man-in-the-street humor, which took comedy out into life, and, of course, his own highly contagious laughter. There was Allen at the news desk, in his battered reporter's hat, when a dam of laughter broke within him. Such was the magic of his breakup that the audience itself became convulsed with laughter. This is typical of Allen's screwball comedy; it is a tragedy that he has not starred in a screwball film comedy. As an actor, oddly enough, he is invariably cast in serious roles (Benny Goodman, George Gershwin, Thomas Paine, etc.).

The life-time schmocking around of Steve Allen has led to the creation of distinctive techniques of comedy. He wrote me that when he was about twelve years old he developed "a certain automatic—almost unconscious—form of humor" that he still involuntarily practices. He starts a sentence in one direction when it dawns upon him there is the possibility of going in a different direction. Talking to Veronica Lake about a feud, he said, "I've heard that there were sparks between you and . . . Ned Sparks." Again, doing "Danny Boy," Steve sang, "Oh, Danny boy . . . the pipes . . . the pipes . . . are leaking."

Steve always has an eye open to the ridiculous in life. He wrote me saying, "Nothing is quite as funny as the unintended humor of reality." As an illustration, Steve sent me a news feature. Discussing Allen's songwriting output, the writer informed us, "At home, he spends much time in his spacious study, where he often turns out as many as three sons a day."

Real life is funny, but Allen can add his antics to real-life situations. In frenetic, booming New York, Steve Allen, live on "The Tonight Show," hails a cab at random. Dressed as a cop, he opens the rear door, tosses in an enormous salami, slams the door and instructs the driver, "Take this to Grand Central Station!" The cab immediately speeds away.

With Steve Allen we can see that it is a signal accomplishment to be creatively silly. Anyone can be silly. But not everyone can be funny when silly.

When Allen is silly he is still in control of events. Playing Superman on the street outside his theatre, Steve got stuck while changing his clothes in the proverbial phone booth, and so just called the first actual passer-by and asked him to help get his pants off.

One of the most important requirements of creative zaniness is that it be natural. With Allen it always is. Allen wrote the lyric for "Picnic" to George Duning's melody but never met him until the song was number one on the Hit Parade. He wrote the lyric for "On the Beach" with composer Ernest Gold before meeting him. One day Gold saw Allen in a parking lot and went over to introduce himself. Steve said, "Go away—it's a better story the other way."

Humor just naturally happens to Steve Allen. This was clear when I had dinner with him at the Brown Derby. When the waiter came over, in near darkness, to take the dinner order, he asked, "What will you have, sir?" Allen answered, "A flashlight."

Allen's natural comic sensibility is ever radiating from his soul; you cannot see him without being touched by it. The total humorous effect, the schmock-schmock factor, always comes across in his action. It is by no means easy to express this intangible comic sensibility in words, and yet this collection does succeed in providing a sense of Allen's great talent. His work is a comedic rainbow containing all of the colors of the humorous spectrum. The whole gamut is represented, from the Milton Berle type of one-liners to the delightful madness of the Marx Brothers, to the profound reflection of Ionesco.

Not only are there several facets of Allen's humor, but there are several Steve Allens. There is the one who writes lyrics and sings songs, who composes music and plays the piano, who is an author of fiction, nonfiction and poetry, who is humanist and humorist, moralist, intellectual and clown, who is not only a Talk Show host but one with the rare quality of knowing how to talk, one we must take seriously, and one who has a genius for not being serious. Who is this man?

Perhaps some mad Kafkan doctor once cloned the real Steve Allen and now there are a dozen of them running about, pretending to be one. But clearly there is a unifying self behind the various talents. That self, very human, expresses itself in a multitude of ways. *The real problem is not that there are too many Steve Allens but that there are too few of the rest of us.*

As most of us do not, Allen uses his creative energy to the fullest, and at the source of it one can always detect a central human core. When Allen was at NBC in the midst of the great competitive wars he announced that he was not worried about his TV rating but about mankind's rating.

In *Always Leave Them Laughing*, Bert Lahr, playing Eddie Egan, insisted that a great comedian must not only make people laugh at him but love him. That was a lesson Kip Cooper, played by Milton Berle, did not learn until almost too late. It is a quality of Steve Allen that he always leaves them laughing without taking leave of his humanity. He mocks the foibles of man, but is always straight about the humanity of man. Behind the many comic masks that Steve Allen wears, in the pages which follow, it is always possible to see a human face.

CONTENTS

SCHMOCK-SCHMOCK!

Chapter One

AFTER DINNER SPEECHES

Most entertainers and authors are upset by ugly comments in a critical review. With Steve Allen it's different. What the critics say about him is usually complimentary. It's what he says about himself that he has to watch out for. The opening words in his autobiography are "I suppose people will read this book who never read the story of Albert Schweitzer, or Galileo, or Robert Owen. They ought to be ashamed of themselves." This is really a man low on vanity and high on intellectual standards. But in this case his judgment is not very good. For *Mark It and Strike It* is a splendid book. In any case, one who could read Albert Schweitzer and Galileo and could not enjoy Steve Allen would be one in whom there was something missing. What is present in Allen is an appreciation for both the sublime *and* the ridiculous. The result is that instead of using his mind to bore us, he uses it to make us laugh heartily. It is this factor that makes him the ideal after-dinner speaker. Not only can he say something funny but he has something relevant to say. Rather than being a specialist, Allen is one who possesses a good general understanding of the world. At one multidisciplinary psychiatric workshop his task was to provide a general summing-up.

1

"Being an expert on nothing that has been discussed here," he said, "I am, of course, the most qualified to discuss everything, because I am uninhibited by those sharply defined professional boundaries that limit the rest of you." Having made that point, Allen continued, "I might be considered in this context a lay expert. No, come to think of it, I'm not even an expert on that. I throw in a bit of vulgarity so that you young people will feel at home."

Allen may not be an expert in any of the social sciences—who is?—but he has an excellent understanding of human nature. His ability to perceive the contradictions in human functioning is a fine weapon for after-dinner wit, as you will observe in the present section.

Most professional comedians arrive at the dinner where they are to entertain with a prepared monologue. Allen is more creative. With him there are three basic approaches.

By one approach, he prepares an address appropriate for the occasion. In the second, Allen's only bag of tricks is himself; he comes to the dinner without knowing at all what he will say. He listens and then decides what he will talk about. He takes notes and these become the basis for his discussion.

Thirdly, he may do a great deal of ad-libbing, and when he does he is at his funniest.

On a Merv Griffin show, astrology being discussed, a woman in the audience asked Allen what sign he was born under. "Furnished rooms for rent," he retorted.

The following material, consisting of Allen's after-dinner speeches, was reconstituted from written routines, transcriptions of tape recordings or from handwritten notes.

REMARKS AT THE MASQUERS' DINNER FOR DEBBIE REYNOLDS (SATURDAY, JUNE 3, 1972)

(Before formal dinners at the Masquers can start, those in attendance must stand, move their chairs, and permit the waiters to take the dinner tables out of the dining room, thus allowing a great many more chairs to be brought in to accommodate the overflow audiences customarily in attendance.

In this instance the crowd was even larger than usual so that the moving of the tables proved a rather noisy and troublesome chore.)

The evening opened with casual, if lengthy, remarks by the dinner chairman, Andy Albin, who made sure that the microphone and public address system were functioning properly, explained the reason for the movement of tables, made small talk, etc.

When quiet had at last been restored, Albin first introduced fellow Masquer Don Randolph, a gentleman with a rich baritone voice, who movingly read the Masquers' Oath. The next speaker was movie producer Jack Warner, who made a few remarks that were unrehearsed and—as usual—somewhat difficult to interpret. His introduction of Mr. Allen was simply as follows ". . . and now here's Steve Allen."

STEVE ALLEN: Thank you, ladies and gentlemen. And I'd like to thank Jack Warner for that highly flattering introduction.

For those of you who have not visited the Masquers before, perhaps I should offer a word of explanation concerning the troublesome movement of tables at the end of the dinner. I never saw such pushing and shoving in my life.

These are the only shows in town that start with a riot.

And even though I've heard it before, I must say I'm always moved by Don Randolph's reading of the Masquers' Oath. Of course Don has such a warm, mellifluous voice that he could read the wording of Proposition 9 and still bring a lump to your throat.

As you will have noted from the printed program, Pat Buttram was supposed to be your Master of Ceremonies this evening, but Pat was unable to join us because something terribly urgent came up for him.

A job.

As regards Andy Albin, copies of his introductory remarks will be available in the lobby after the dinner. In the form of a long-playing album.

Actually, it's entirely understandable that Andy is a nervous

3

wreck this evening. I doubt if you have any idea how much work, how much worry, how much energy goes into planning an affair of this sort. The biggest problem Andy had, of course, was booking all the top stars and performers whom you see on the dais.

Frankly, I don't know why we have to go to so much trouble. I don't know why they just don't send Debbie to lunch with Frank Gorshin and let it go at that.

As is customary at dinners of this sort, a number of congratulatory wires have been received, but I don't think we ought to take time to read them aloud. I just happened to have noticed this one from Phyllis Diller.

Incidentally, if her famous face lift was so successful, how come we can still recognize her?

By the way, I wonder if we can turn off this noisy air conditioner right over my head. It sounds like a fan in a Chinese restaurant I was once thrown out of in Chicago.

Perhaps I should explain next that I was called only a couple of days ago to replace Pat Buttram and therefore my notes are in a rather chaotic order. As a matter of fact, the papers before me on the lectern probably shouldn't be called notes at all. They look literally like the contents of a wastebasket.

And I'm having a bit of a problem with the cards that were given to me by Andy Albin. They're terribly small. Three or four of them seem to be on microfilm.

As you can see, I'm quite nearsighted. In fact, I'm so nearsighted I have to wear contact lenses to see my glasses.

And if Andy thinks this piece of paper (he holds paper aloft) is any help, he's out of his mind. As you can see, it's in Andy's own handwriting and I want you to know that he left school in third grade . . . to go on the Pantages Time.

Now, as I analyze the list of names of people who are to be introduced, it seems to break down into three categories.

1) Consists of people who are to be introduced.
2) Consists of people who do *not* wish to be introduced.
3) Is a list of people who are *determined* to be introduced.

One of those present in the audience is one of Hollywood's loveliest actresses, with whom I had the pleasure of co-starring in *The Benny Goodman Story*, Miss Donna Reed.

Besides being a fine actress, Donna is also a very active citizen. She is one of the leaders, as you may know, in that fine organization "Women For."

I saw her talking the other day to Rona Barrett, who's connected with "Women Against."

(A number of other formal introductions were made at this point.)

And also out there is a former leading welterweight, who recently served as technical adviser on *The Great White Hope*, Mr. Mushy Callahan.

Mushy, yours has always sounded to me like the name of a health-food cereal. You know, something like "Crunchy Granola."

Also in the audience tonight we have a gentleman named Rudy Render, who I understand accompanies Debbie.

That is, he accompanies her on the *piano*.

He is, in any event, her arranger. He arranges her music, her hair, whatever needs arranging.

Perhaps next I should explain that some other friends of Debbie's would be here this evening except that on this same night the B'Nai B'Rith of Beverly Hills is holding the Aaron Spelling Dinner at the Hilton Hotel.

Which explains why we have so many gentiles here this evening.

Incidentally, before we go any further, I must stop and bring to your attention the delightful picture of Debbie on the cover of this evening's program. There's something unique about this photograph, something that I doubt that you appreciate. All the rest of us performers—actors, singers, dancers, night-club entertainers, whatever—we all have to have new pictures taken every few years. You can't go on using the same old 8 by 10 glossies because every few years there comes the time when you look at your picture and say, "I don't look like that any more."

But in Debbie's case, she has *always* looked like this. She looked like this when she was four years old. And she will look like this, no doubt, when she is an old woman.

5

Which she may already be, for all that we have any way of knowing.

By the way, if you'll consult your program, you'll notice that there are a number of people whose appearance was advertised, but who are in fact not here. Mayor Yorty, for example, is not here.

But then he rarely is.

You know, we professional comedians have a particular fondness for Sam Yorty. As far as we're concerned, he's sort of a walking straight-line.

I think he's criticized too much. I mean, people are constantly blaming him for everything that's wrong with Los Angeles. They blame him for the smog, they blame him for traffic problems, they blame him for corruption. Now I ask you, how could he be responsible for these things when he's never here?

But he does have tough luck. He got into trouble this week with McGovern and Humphrey. And it's affected him too. Two fellows at the bar downstairs here at the Masquers were having a heated discussion last night. I heard one of them say, "Now let's be gentlemanly about this and discuss the matter fairly. You go first."

Yorty came running up and said, "Wait, I want in on this."

Some people say that Yorty had greatness thrust upon him.

And he ducked.

This cold blast of air over my head is beginning to annoy me. From the front I've got lights on me hot enough to fade my suit, and in the back I'm being hit by the air from an icebox. The whole thing is making me very ill at ease.

Actually, I haven't been this nervous since the guy at C&R Clothiers measured my inseam.

Well, Debbie, are you having fun? That's good. But I want you to remember this: The Masquers gave me one of these dinners one time—and I didn't work for two years.

By the way, ladies and gentlemen, we're actually quite lucky that Debbie herself is here with us this evening. Joe Pasternak is ill, Meredith Willson is ill, and just a few days ago Debbie thought she had mononucleosis. But her husband, Harry, pulled a few strings, and now I'm glad to report she has *stereo*-nucleosis.

6

In that connection you might recall having read, about a week ago, that she had to cancel out of her show in Las Vegas one night because of a pinched nerve.

Ladies and gentlemen, I happen to know who pinched it.

Well, now it's time to introduce more of the distinguished people on the dais. First, I think I should refer to those who will *not* be speaking. I'm glad that *some* of them are not speaking or this dinner would wind up being a communion breakfast.

The first lady who will not have anything to say is the *wife* of one of Debbie's good friends in the industry, the famed Warner Brothers talent scout, Solly Biano.

(At this point *Mr.* Biano stood up, came to the microphone and, visibly very nervous, said a few words. The lectern was set up on a small piano and during Biano's remarks one of the keys sounded loudly.)

STEVE: Well, as you can see, ladies and gentlemen, things have gone all to hell. I thought *I* was nervous. Solly Biano was so nervous he thought he was *Mrs.* Biano.

And did you notice that while he was speaking you heard a note from the piano. Actually, Solly's whole body was rigid with fear and the weird thing about that note was that he didn't strike it with his hands.

(A *few other speakers were introduced.*)

Now I'd like you to meet one of the most literate, charming and witty women in our industry. Pamela, what is the name of your latest book?

PAMELA: *The Female Pleasure Hunt.*

STEVE: Ah, yes. She saw the need for the book when she saw that her seventy-year old milkman wasn't delivering like he used to.

STEVE: Ladies and gentlemen, Pamela Mason.

By the way, I hope you all turn your eyes to the left and look at that remarkable set for the play that's currently being presented at the Masquers, A *Frog He Would A-Wooing Go.* Actually the set is an exact replica of George Burns's old room at the Edison Hotel.

But it's a great play, and I urge you to see it.

Incidentally, Masquers: Do you want your shows here to play to standing room only?

Take out the seats.

Oh, I just realized that I've overlooked introducing a very important guest in the audience. He's a member of the Masquers' Club, and I know they're all very proud of him this week.

I'm talking, of course, about Mr. A. C. Thomas.

Yesterday morning Mr. Thomas touched a live wire carrying fourteen thousand volts.

A. C. Thomas is now D. C. Thomas.

(At this point Agnes Moorehead and Lillian Burns Sidney, George Sidney, Ernest Borgnine, Pat O'Brien, Jack Haley and director George Marshall were introduced.)

There are a few young people here this evening, but I think one of the reasons this is such a warm, genial occasion is that we have so many marvelous faces in the room that we have been enjoying for so many years. A lot of us here go back to the old days in Hollywood, back to the days when Hot Pants was a condition.

Just think of it, ladies and gentlemen, on Hollywood Boulevard not far from where we are, we have the stars' names lying on the sidewalk. In the old days the stars *themselves* were lying on the sidewalk.

Together.

And I'm talking about Ramon Navarro and Laird Cregar.

Next, a gentleman who is one of our industry's most distinguished producers. Do you remember the wonderful film *Bitter Rice?* Well, he didn't produce that.

But he did a picture very much like it called *Rancid Oatmeal*.

This gentleman, unquestionably, has charisma. He also has asthma.

Mr. Arthur Freed.

Next, I'd like to introduce one of our great comediennes.

Years ago I remember that people were impressed that Martha Raye was—how shall I say this?—well endowed up front. And a lot of people remarked on what a small waist she had. Pat Buttram said it was very easy to understand. Nothing grows very much when it's in the shade all the time.

(Martha Raye then entertained for a few minutes, resorting, as is her custom, to various anatomical references, pasting bits of toilet paper to her eyebrows, etc.)

Thank you, Martha. I'd like to announce, ladies and gentlemen, that Martha Raye has just been honored with the Dame May Whitty Award for "Lady-like Behavior under Stress."

I always enjoy visiting the Masquers. It's so relaxed and home-like. Last week I had dinner here one night. I said to the waiter, "I'll have the roast beef with natural gravy."

He said, "Where do you see that?"

I said, "On your tie."

When the hell are we going to get that cold *air* turned off?

Pat O'Brien just gave an Irish toast, "May the wind be always at your back . . ." Well, this wind is at *my* back and I'm getting pretty sick of it.

And now, a bit of information about our guest of honor.

While working for the Girl Scouts, Debbie handled bookkeeping chores. Her boss instructed her to always add a column of figures *three times* before showing him the results.

The next day Debbie proudly presented him with an itemized report of expenditures. "Oh, chief," she said, "I added these figures *ten* times."

"That's wonderful," her boss said. "I like a girl to be thorough."

"Thank you," Debbie said, "here are my ten *answers*."

In 1948, Debbie entered the Miss Burbank Contest, which is interesting, because it's apparently the first time in history that we have documentary evidence that anybody ever actually *did* miss Burbank.

But in that contest she won a prize for an imitation of Betty Hutton.

The runner-up was Betty Hutton, who imitated Debbie Reynolds.

9

A Warner Brothers talent scout signed Debbie to a role in *The Daughter of Rosie O'Grady*, after which she played the part of Helen Kane, the boop-a-doop girl of the early 1930s, in *Three Little Words*.

I know from my own experience that when it is said that such-and-such an actor appeared in such-and-such a picture, somehow there's the impression that the actor had a *big* role in the picture. In *this* case, probably Debbie herself doesn't remember whether she played a large or small part in these two films, but there's a story that makes the same point.

A certain character actor (who hadn't worked in a few years) was called in to read for the part of the doctor in *A Streetcar Named Desire*.

If you remember that marvelous film you'll recall that the doctor doesn't even show *up* until the last few *seconds* of the picture. All he has to do is take poor Blanche away to the hospital.

Well, the actor was so excited at getting a job that he couldn't wait to talk about it when he ran into a friend on the street.

He said, "Hey, I just landed the part of the *doctor* in *A Streetcar Named Desire*.

"That's great," his friend said. "What's the picture about?"

"Well," the actor said, "it's about this *doctor*, and one day he . . ."

One of the high spots of Debbie's career came in 1965, when she starred in M-G-M's *The Singing Nun*.

That picture was such a success that she immediately made a sequel to it called *The Whistling Rabbi*.

I'm referring again to her biography here. It says, "A native of El Paso, Texas, she lived in that city until the age of eight."

Which is as long as anybody should live in El Paso.

"Then her father, who worked for the Southern Pacific Railroad, was transferred to Southern California."

Actually he wasn't *transferred*; he was *sidetracked*.

In closing I'd like to sing a little noncomic song I've written about Debbie, especially for this occasion.

DEBBIE

Princes and kings
Have said wonderful things
    about Debbie.
Ev'ryday folks
Love the laughter and jokes
    that she brings.

You must admit
There's a sparkle—a wit
    about Debbie.
No other girl we know
Has quite that certain glow.

Bon mot or blooper,
She's always a trouper,
    our Debbie.
If you're in a spot
There are some who will not
    pull you through.

But she's the Queen of them all;
She's our Belle of the Ball
We don't mean mebbe,
Oh, Debbie,
We all love you.

REMARKS AT THE MASQUERS' DINNER FOR PEARL BAILEY (OCTOBER 2, 1970)

I'd like to thank your harlequin for that lengthy introduction, which I so richly required. (Lately, I've been involved in so many things, I'm not sure who the hell I am any more.) But this is a big evening and I'm about as nervous as Tiny Tim on his honeymoon night. I know what I'm supposed to *do*—I'm just not sure I'm *up* to it.

I'm a last-minute substitute. Originally, the Masquers wanted someone else to fill this spot . . . that fine comedian, John Cameron Swayze. Unfortunately, Mr. Swayze couldn't be here. He's busy running around the country looking for strange things to strap watches on. Like Don Rickles' tongue.

Their next choice was that popular rustic philosopher, Pat Buttram (the Myra Breckenridge of the Harper Valley PTA), but Pat's busy, too. He's up in Santa Barbara, helping Ronnie Reagan pour troubled waters on the *oil.*

Many of you have made a great sacrifice to be here tonight—you're missing the rerun of *Gilligan's Island* on Channel 13. A great movie on Channel 5, starring Lex Barker and Chili Williams . . . the "Harry Joe Brown Film Festival" on Channel 11 . . . and that great documentary on Channel 9 . . . *The Part the Vatican Plays in the Used Car Racket.*

George Jessel was supposed to be here tonight, but he had to go to Vietnam. To get his toupe defoliated.

I've been to Vietnam myself and I know how important it is that our troops there get good entertainment. But have you ever stopped to think how little sense it makes to send Jessel over there? The average young American soldier is either a nineteen-year-old hillbilly from Arkansas, a twenty-year-old Negro from Alabama, or a twenty-one-year-old Mexican from San Antonio. I swear to God, none of these men know what the hell Jessel is talking about.

Hal Kanter wanted to be here tonight but he had to stay out at the studio. Something big has come up. *Raymond Massey* put on his old *shawl* and *stovepipe hat* and went out to 20th to free the cast of "Julia."

I happen to know for a fact that when Hal Kanter began casting the TV series "Julia" he offered the script to Pearl Bailey. When she turned it down, he signed Lloyd Nolan for the part.

Anyway, we are here to honor a great lady, a star who is a member of a minority group—beautiful women.

She's also *working,* which, show business being in the shape it's in today, is a *real* minority.

Your chairman *Frank Scannel* said the club wanted to honor

her even before 20th Century-Fox did, and when I asked him how *Fox* had honored her, he looked surprised. "Didn't you see *Tora! Tora! Tora!?*" he asked me. "It's all about the Japanese attack on Pearl."

I told him that was Pearl Harbor. He said, "When'd she change her name?" And Scannel is this club's leading intellectual.

One great thing about Pearlie, she has *never* had to use blue material to make audiences laugh. I remember when you couldn't say *"heck"* on television or you'd get in trouble. Now on TV, on Broadway and in night clubs . . . every place . . . they use every *four-letter word* in the book. Maybe I'm old-fashioned, but . . . any comedian who insists that he *has* to use dirt and filth and vulgarity to get a laugh . . . I say to him, *"Bullshit!"*

And I say to Jan Murray, "Thanks for the joke."

Broadway is going to hell, too. Pearl Bailey was sensational in *Hello, Dolly.* Now David Merrick says he may give the part to Liberace.

I'm not surprised, when they're making movies about lesbians, homosexuals, wife swappers. Why, it's gotten so bad I was afraid to take my kids to see *Chitty Chitty Bang Bang.* It sounded dirty to *me.*

Things have gotten so bad the censors are threatening to give an X rating to that new Walt Disney nature movie unless they cut out some of the footage of two bald eagles making it in mid-air over Topanga Canyon.

But it's wonderful how much *freedom* there is in show business today.

It's just great when a *black woman* can play a part written for a *white woman*, as in *Hello, Dolly.* Then a white man . . . Liberace . . . can play the *same part.* I mean, there are no rules any more.

There may be a remake of *Going My Way*, with Pearl playing Bing's part.

Pearl Bailey has really looked beautiful tonight . . . In fact, when she walked in she looked so great I thought it was Flip Wilson in drag.

13

When Pearl Bailey comes out on a stage she really is the second most beautifully gowned woman in show business. My *first* vote still goes to *Milton Berle*.

You know, there's very little you can *kid* Pearl Bailey about . . . I can't say she's a *drunk* . . . or she's a *drug* addict . . . or she's a *sex fiend*.

I can't, but maybe *she'll* tell you about that later.

I think everybody in our business has loved Pearl Bailey. Where she found the time I have no idea.

My *respect* for Pearl has *grown* over the years. But then so has Pearl.

We all naturally have *admiration* and great *affection* for this lady, but no matter who you are, or what you do in this business, there are always some people who will *criticize* you. For example, some of the brothers have recently said that, although Pearl is a great talent, she isn't doing enough for the young black radicals. Naturally, Pearl feels this kind of criticism very *deeply*. So, just to balance the scales tonight, she is going to sing two choruses of Stokely Carmichael's "Star Dust."

I must mention the hallmark of Pearl Bailey's style of performing. She takes it easy.

I'm supposed to be a pretty relaxed performer, but Pearl tops me by a mile. She is so relaxed she makes Perry Como look like Tom Jones.

In fact, she's gotten more and more casual over the years, to the point that right in the middle of her act on my show one night she was arrested for loitering.

In my capacity as a songwriter, she's been very kind to me. Years ago she recorded one of my songs called "What Happened to the Hair on the Head of the Man I Love?" Even then she sang so slow that before she had gotten to the second chorus I had received over eight hundred dollars in royalties.

And she's married to a great guy, who is one of the great drummers of all time, Mr. Louie Belson. I'll tell you a fascinating thing about Louie's own family. Not only is his a happy interracial marriage, but one of his brothers, Harry, is also married to a wonderful Negro woman.

14

Louie has four other brothers. All of them have been divorced except Louis and Harry.

You know, Jessel does these dinners in honor of people he's never even met. But I'm glad to be able to say that I've known Pearl Bailey for a good many years. Today she's an institution, but I first knew her when she was a singer.

Listen, I knew her when she was colored.

That may seem like just a dumb joke . . . and it was, but there was more meaning to it than might appear on the surface because there is a sense in which we don't think of Pearl as black, white or any other color. We just think of her as a very wonderful human being. Which is as it should be.

INTRODUCTION TO JOE PASTERNAK

People have made a lot of poor-taste jokes about Joe Pasternak for no other reason than that he is Hungarian. People think that Hungarians are all gypsies—that Hungarians are less honest than other ethnic groups. As regards Joe Pasternak, well, I can only tell you about something that he did the other day when he accidentally backed into somebody else's parked car on the lot at Universal.

He got out, wrote a note and left it on the other driver's windshield. I happened to be there at the time. I went over and read that note and I have it here. This is what Joe wrote:

"Dear Sir, I have just run into your car. People have seen me and are watching me write this. They think I am giving you my name and address. They are wrong."

Thirty years ago, when I was just getting started in this business, one of the first people to try to borrow money from me was this Hungarian, Joe Pasternak. He said, "Can I borrow fifty dollars?"

I said, "Joe, lending money often spoils a good friendship, and ours is worth a lot more than fifty bucks."

He said, "All right, make it a hundred."

Joe Pasternak's success story is truly remarkable. He came to this country a poor young man, but right from the start he was resourceful. When he rented his first room here in Hollywood the landlord knocked on his door one day and asked for the rent.

"I'm sorry," Joe said, "I haven't got it."

"But listen," the landlord said, "for the past month you've been promising to give it to me."

"Well, all right," Joe said. "If I promised you the rent I'll give it to you."

"But when?" the landlord said.

"Ah," Joe replied, "that I couldn't promise."

They say that Pasternak's movies were light and frothy and escapist, but I say, what's wrong with that? Actually Joe's first job with the old Universal Studio was reading all the scripts that came in. It was his business to separate the chaff from the wheat, and then make movies out of the chaff.

It's great to see Joe in good health again. I'm sure you remember hearing the recent reports about his physical condition, and you probably all read about the strange symptoms that he suffered from. He used to shake, tremble and feel depressed. But, Joe, don't you realize that thousands of men in this town have had those same symptoms just from talking to Jack Warner?

Ladies and gentlemen—your harlequin—Joe Pasternak.

VARIETY CLUB LUNCHEON FOR SAMMY DAVIS, JR. (FEBRUARY 2, 1972) (Audience Consisting of Motion Picture Exhibitors, Distributors, etc., Beverly Hills)

Thank you very much, Gary Owen, Sammy, Senator Gravel and distinguished visitors.

It's a great pleasure to address you exhibitionists.

And I think the very fact that you're present at this carefree occasion today is a great tribute to your good nature, inasmuch as a number of you are presently being sued by the major film companies.

I am pleased to participate in this tribute to Sammy today because I have known him for a very long time. Back in 1949, when

I was doing a radio show here in the CBS studios in Hollywood, he used to come into the studio, sit on top of the piano, sing, dance and make the same great impression that he still makes on audiences.

I recall that just a few days before that I had gone to a little club here in town called The Palms. I believe it was on Western Avenue; is that right, Sam?

Yes. I remember I went into this little broken-down night club and I saw a remarkable act. A middle-aged man dancing with his son, a teen-age boy. I remember saying to myself, "That old guy's *got* something."

Which reminds me that yesterday they showed the Benny Goodman Story again on television. It was Sammy Davis, Sr., who played the part of Fletcher Henderson in that picture.

I can't mention in mixed company which part of Fletcher Henderson he played, but . . .

Incidentally, that was a very interesting lunch we just had. I've never tasted meat like that before. Since this is a brand-new hotel, they're naturally still having trouble with the service, so some of us had our luncheon catered from the Saddle and Sirloin Room. Unfortunately I got the saddle.

By the way, Gary, a number of people wanted to know where Max Kaplan, the head of Mattell Toys, was sitting. He neglected to stand up when you introduced him. For those of you who are interested, Mr. Kaplan is the gentleman sitting right over there. With the key in his back.

In case my face looks odd . . . I fell asleep under a sun lamp this morning and got a little burn.

Another half an hour and this luncheon could have been given for me.

I'm so glad to see Sammy's lovely wife, Edelweiss, or Axlegrease or Malt-o-Meal? Whatever.

Sammy is not only an American star. He's an international star. Like a Maurice Chevalier or a Danny Kaye. He's at home all over Europe. When he's in London he enjoys dining at the Ritz, dancing at the Dorchester, stompin' at the Savoy.

And Sammy knows how to handle the enormous sums of money he's earned. He doesn't flaunt his wealth, but on the other hand he spends as if to the manor born. In Europe—you know the House of Rothschild? He just bought the house.

Sammy is a great photographer, you know. And he's smart about it. On the first box of film he ever bought he noticed it said "Keep in a Cool Place." He kept it at Birdland.

Sammy has shown great social courage. He hasn't been afraid to take a stand on the big issues. For example, there was the case of the Los Angeles Country Club which, as you know, was very restricted. When Sammy found out they didn't accept actors, Jews or Negroes he applied for membership . . . and was turned down three times.

It isn't easy being black and Jewish at the same time. I'm reminded of the unfortunate incident several months ago in New York when there was trouble between the Negroes and the Jews. Both sides asked Sammy to take a stand. So he slapped himself in the mouth.

And he is very sincere about his conversion to Judaism. He walked off my show last week rather than take a taste of Jimmy Dean Pork Sausage.

You know, it's a funny thing about race. If you don't know a man very well, sometimes the factor of race seems important. But I've known Sammy for over twenty years, and he's such a good, personal friend that sometimes to me he seems almost colored.

But he is a man of principle. And he's deeply religious. He is the only man I know who personally believed in the Second Coming of Howard Hughes.

And he has political courage, too. He was the first man in our industry to stand up and say, "Vote No on Preparation H."

They say Sam has thrown away a lot of his money. All I know is: A little while ago before lunch he had to take out a Teamster's Pension-Fund loan to leave a tip for the guy in the men's room.

Another fine thing about Sam is that he has a good head for business. You probably read the item in one of the trade paper columns the other day to the effect that he is part of the television syndicate which will be importing and reproducing successful American television shows to Israel. Because of Sammy's great popularity over there, his judgment about such things is naturally much respected.

I understand that the only revision Sammy plans to make in some of these TV series is to change the names.

If you're going to be in television for the next year you might look for the following shows:

1. "Gun Schmuck"
2. "Star Dreck"
3. That wonderfully exciting legal series called "Jew for the Defense."
4. "The Ghost and Mrs. Meyer"
5. Perry Mason over there will be called "*Jackie* Mason."
6. "Gentile Ben"
7. "Hawaii $49.94"
8. Sammy has booked the Galloping Gourmet. Over there it will be called "Eat it . . . You'll like it."
9. "Monday Night at the Movies" will be changed to "Tuesday Night at the Shulmans'."
10. "I Dream of Julius."
11. "The Man From Yonkle."
12. And lastly, "Batman" will be changed to "Batman and Sons."

REMARKS AT OPENING OF SCOPE AUDITORIUM, NORFOLK, VIRGINIA
(NOVEMBER 13, 1971)

VOICE ON PUBLIC-ADDRESS SYSTEM: And now . . . Mr. Steve Allen.

Good evening, ladies and gentleman. I don't know whose voice it was who just introduced me, but I'd like to thank the gentleman for that very flattering introduction.

I hope I have the opportunity to return the favor sometime.

But I must say that it has been a most enjoyable experience visiting your wonderful city. The warm welcome started the moment I got off the plane this morning when Mayor Martin ran up and presented me with Norfolk's Mace.

I just wish he hadn't sprayed it directly into my eyes.

It was also most gratifying when I came into the auditorium this evening to see a group of hippies giving me the peace sign.

One finger at a time.

Although the existence of Scope is naturally of enormous importance here in Norfolk, if you'll forgive me I had heard nothing about it three thousand miles away in Los Angeles until just recently. In fact, when I first received the invitation from Scope, I thought I was being booked to appear at a mouthwash convention.

This place is really fabulous, and it's not even finished yet. They plan to have not just great entertainment here, but sometimes four and five shows going on in different areas simultaneously. Even tonight they have this wonderful "Spirit of America" musical in this room, there's a rock band rehearsing in Chrysler Hall, there's a Latin combo in the Little Hall, you can hear taped music in the parking lot, and they have entertainment going on in the restaurant.

Would you believe it, I went into the men's room a few minutes ago. They've got a six-piece band working in there.

Don't laugh . . . they were getting a standing ovation.

This auditorium is equipped to put on full-scale shows of any sort, as you'll see in a little while, and the Tidewater area can be proud of it.

Of course, there are a few little technical problems. For example, at the moment my dressing-room backstage seems to be full of tidewater.

And wait till you see this great "Spirit of America" show. It's really something. You'll see literally hundreds of fighting men, the Army chorus, the Army band. They'll re-create the War of 1812, the attack on Fort Sumter, battle action from the War with Mexico.

And these men really put their all into the show, too. After it's over, they don't just go home to bed; they attack Virginia Beach!

I don't think there's ever been a show like the "Spirit of America." You'll see British soldiers pitted against American colonials. You'll see covered wagons racing to open the West. You'll see rugged cavalrymen fighting off hostile Indians.

You'll see Johnny Carson beaten senseless by Ed McMahon.

You'll see Senator Fulbright answering an obscene phone call from Martha Mitchell.

And—if you'll refer to your programs—you'll notice that it says, "To top it all off, there'll be spectacular fireworks following the show."

It wasn't planned that way, but we've been having a little trouble with the electrical system.

Speaking of the program, I do hope you've studied it carefully, because it gives you such fascinating information about this fabulous Scope project. Let me direct your attention to a few of the high spots.

"It might be said that Scope grew out of a basic need and a late-night phone call . . . from Mr. Lawrence M. Cox in Washington, D.C., to Mayor Roy B. Martin."

Collect.

Mr. Cox, then executive director of the Norfolk Redevelopment and Housing Authority, said it might be possible to include the construction of a new center in Norfolk in the 1965 Federal Housing and Urban Development Act. This has meant that the federal government, as part of Norfolk's over-all Urban Renewal program, pays two thirds of the final construction costs whereas the city of Norfolk pays only one third.

How Harry Byrd justified this in his mind I have no idea.

The project was designed by the Williams and Tazewell Partnership of Norfolk, and this fabulous dome roof over our heads was the concept of the famed Italian architect, Señor Nervi.

And when they got the bill from him, they saw why he was called Nervy.

But just look at that roof. It doesn't have one visible inch of supporting structure, but it's very safe and strong.

I hope to God.

21

No, seriously, it is very strong. But I do suggest that you do not all cough at once.

The program goes on to say, "The structure of Scope is essentially a very large boat. It is in a real sense like an iceberg. . . ." Some critics predict that it will either sink or melt.

The structure is well below the water table. It extends down as much as fifteen feet below ground water. Four thousand concrete piles stabilize the project.

And, ladies and gentlemen, these piles are surrounded by 249 square feet of Preparation H.

The floor slab is about three feet thick and there are more than two million seven hundred thousand cubic feet of concrete overall. This is enough concrete to build a sidewalk four hundred miles long.

Which is just long enough to help you walk back to your car after the show.

And you will pay particular attention, after the show this evening, to the lower concourse. You will notice that the program advises us, "There are sunken gardens on either side of the lower entry." Think of it, ladies and gentlemen, sunken gardens. They didn't *plan* it that way; it's just that there was a little problem with the cement.

But whether those gardens sank or not, they're still beautiful.

The handsome restaurant and cocktail lounge seats 240 persons. And sleeps 75.

Next is a storage area and parking space for the "zamboni," the machine that keeps the surface of the ice smooth.

Actually it's not a machine; it's an old Italian guy named Zamboni.

The ice rink, located in the arena floor here, has twenty-two miles of steel tubing buried in the concrete and will provide ice not only for professional hockey, but also for drinking.

Extensive landscaping enhances the brick-paved plaza and is a focal point for a large reflecting pool.

It is three inches deep.

Who the wise guy was who put the diving board at one end, we do not know.

One of the world's most advanced electronic scoreboards will provide a dazzling display of lighted information. It is one of the nation's biggest.

Although the scores here won't be that big, I understand. But you will be able to see great sports events here. All the local athletes and coaches are thrilled. Particularly Johnny Wilson, new coach of the Wings hockey team. I was just reading in the program that Johnny was the winner of the Calder Cup. Apparently Calder himself decided not to wear it any more.

But Johnny is terrific. He earned the nickname "Iron Man" when he played 580 consecutive National Hockey League games. Unfortunately, Johnny does not remember the last 107 games.

The scoreboard was built by American Sign and Indicator Corporation of Spokane, Washington. There is just one little problem. They have to fly a guy in from three thousand miles to change a light bulb.

Continuing with the printed program here you will notice that "The air-conditioning plant at Scope is large enough to comfortably cool 500 average-sized homes."

It's enough to give me penumonia at the moment, but I didn't come here to complain.

"Individual temperature readings in the various areas can be monitored and adjusted," at a central control station, conveniently located in Birmingham, Alabama.

And notice this announcement: "An emergency power system was designed to provide emergency lighting within eight seconds, should the primary source of power fail."

So if everything suddenly goes dark here tonight, ladies and gentlemen, remember: You have exactly seven seconds to wild it up.

Speaking of that sort of thing, I direct your attention to the forty very attractive young ladies who will serve as usherettes at the various sports and entertainment events here.

As you will see by the program, the ensemble they wear is made of polyester double knit and features navy hot pants.

Frankly, I don't see what's so special about that. The Navy has had hot pants for years.

One really unusual thing is that "The fashions were selected by Miss Sarah Higginbotham, an interior designer for the Williams and Tazewell Partnership architectural firm. So far as I know, this is the first time that women's clothing has been designed by an architect. It's worked out pretty well except for one little problem: The undergarments are made of cement.

Lastly, I suppose I should say a word about a point that has been the subject, I understand, of considerable controversy here in Norfolk during the last few years. There is just no denying the fact that the total cost of Scope itself, as the program tells you, was twenty-eight million dollars.

If we include tips and bribes, it came to forty-nine million, but what the hell.

At the first show last evening I introduced quite a number of dignitaries. I think the number was 497. At the moment, the only dignitary present is your vice mayor, Mr. V. H. Nusbaum, Jr. It's interesting that you would have a mayor for that, too.

And now . . . on with the show.

REMARKS AT THE FRIARS' CLUB DINNER FOR BILL HARBACH AND NICK VANOFF (JANUARY 30, 1965)

Tony Martin, master of ceremonies for the evening—which included comedy entertainment by Mel Brooks, Carl Reiner, Bill "Jose Jimenez" Dana, George Burns, and Corbett Monica—introduced Allen as "a man who had the good sense to buy Polaroid at twelve."

Thank you, Tony, and good evening, ladies and gentlemen.

Yes, as you've been told, I did buy Polaroid at twelve. Unfortunately I *sold* it when I was fourteen, like an idiot.

But I'm extremely happy to be here this evening to pay my respects to two such close friends. We worked together for so many years and I have benefited greatly by their support. In fact,

I've often gotten credit for things that they were responsible for. It was Nick Vanoff, for example, who actually discovered Andy Williams and Carol Burnett.

He discovered them in the back seat of a parked car.

But these two men are successful today, and they deserve their success. You can always tell, of course, when people have that certain something. I am reminded of the day, almost fifteen years ago, when two young men came to me just bursting with good ideas. They had great energy, a lot of ability. I knew they were going places. I'm talking about Panama and Frank. What happened to Harbach and Vanoff after that meeting I have no idea.

But—seriously—it's wonderful to see these two fellows working together so effectively when they come from such different backgrounds. Think of it. These two young men, one of whom is from the wrong side of the tracks, the other of whom *owns* the tracks. . . .

Now, of course, you all know that Bill's father is the great American songwriter Otto Harbach. But what some of you may not know is that Nick's father was the great *Macedonian* songwriter Otto Vanoff.

You all know the wonderful songs written by Bill's father, but let me tell you about Nick's father.

Bill's father wrote "The Indian Love Call."

Nick's father wrote "The Armenian Love Call."

Bill's father wrote "Smoke Gets in Your Eyes."

Nick's father wrote "Smoke Gets in Your Nose."

And he wrote it first!

Bill's father wrote "You Do Something to Me."

Nick's father wrote "I'll Do Something to You."

Bill's father wrote "The Touch of Your Hand."

Nick's father wrote "Your Feet Are Like Ice."

Bill's father wrote "Rosemarie."

Nick's father wrote "Morey Amsterdam."

Jayne and I have known Bill since his early days as a young fledgling actor, when the two of them worked at M-G-M. In fact, that was Bill's professional name in those days, Fledgling Young. He didn't want to make it on his father's reputation. But his story is inspiring. He came to Hollywood, ladies and gentlemen, without a penny in his pocket. But with fifty thousand dollars in his briefcase.

Now I know that's an old joke. But Bill is no spring chicken himself.

You know, when I met these fellows they had already done great things in the early days of television. In New York, Bill had produced the "Jean Martin Show," "The Nick Kenny Show," and the "Late Weather Report with Nancy Berg." These were milestones, ladies and gentlemen.

And at this same time, in Hollywood, Nick was producing the "N.T.G. Bathing Beauty Parade," "Peter Potter's Platter Parade," and the "Roller Derby." Remember that great program "You Asked for It"? Well, Nick was doing a horror show called "It Asked for You."

But it's a wonderful tribute, not only to these two men, but to our American way of life, that a wealthy young man from Park Avenue could work side by side for all these years with a poor Macedonian *immigrant*. But Bill is very graceful about his wealth. And so is his lovely wife, Faye. I remember seeing her with their first child several years ago as they sat in the back seat of a limousine on Park Avenue. The little girl was just a year and a half old at the time. I said, "Can she walk?" and Faye said, "Thank God she'll never have to!"

Today Bill and Faye have *two* fine children, and, like their parents, they're not at all spoiled by being so rich. Last Christmas their oldest little girl walked up to Santa Claus and said, "What can I do for you?"

But—seriously—Faye and Bill live a very simple life. They don't keep servants. They *hire* a lot of them, but they don't keep them.

And once again I say "but seriously," and this time I mean it, when I express my pleasure at being here this evening to be part of this program that is meant to convey the admiration and deep affection all of us feel for Bill Harbach and Nick Vanoff.

26

REMARKS AT THE MOTION PICTURE HOME LUNCHEON FOR SAM
GOLDWYN (JUNE 26, 1966)

Since I feel it is important to let you know exactly what you are
in for I would like to briefly read to you from the agenda,
with which I have been provided.

I will not be taking a great deal of your time because my
primary function here this afternoon is to introduce the various
distinguished visitors who grace our dais. Each of them, I believe,
will address you. When that has been done I will reintroduce
you to Mr. Bagnall, who in turn will introduce Mr. Goldwyn.
It will then be my pleasure to invite all of you to proceed outside
for the dedication of the Plaza.

What is going to take place out there specifically is that another dais will be set up, on which will be seated, I presume, the
same group I will have already introduced you to in here. They
will rise and address you again. If there are any jokes you do not
understand the first time around, therefore, it looks as if you are
going to have the opportunity to get a second crack at them.

To *conclude* the Plaza dedication ceremonies Mr. Bagnall will
once again introduce Mr. Goldwyn, who will presumably rise
to the occasion with a clarification of his earlier remarks.

You will then be permitted to . . . uh . . . finger the wet
cement out there for a few minutes.

Promptly at three, I am informed by this run-down, the annual
meeting will get under way. The annual meeting of *what* I have
no idea.

But, whatever it is, it will be called to order by Mr. Bagnall,
who then—by virtue of his vast experience acquired at these two
out-of-town tryouts—should really be warmed up and clicking
right along.

If the annual meeting proves to be the million laughs that it
figures to be, I confidently predict that Jules Stein will sell it to
Jack Warner as a TV series. Playing the part of Mr. Bagnall will

be someone who is more the public image of the executive: Lucille Ball. And within thirteen weeks—I further predict—it will be canceled by Tom Sarnoff here.

Regarding the dedication of the new Plaza, a further word: As those of you who are intimates of Mr. Goldwyn are aware, he is notorious for his poor memory for names. In fact, I have had personal experience that establishes to my satisfaction that this part of the Goldwyn myth, at least, is grounded in fact.

When I first had the pleasure of meeting Mr. Goldwyn, about four years ago, I spent an enjoyable afternoon in his company. During the course of our conversation he confided that he had enjoyed my television program on a number of occasions. I was naturally flattered and was additionally pleased to discover that, because he referred to particular sketches, he was not indulging in empty flattery. His praise, in fact, would have gone to my head were it not for the fact that as I left his home he said, "Keep up the good work, Ed."

Well, as I say, his closest friends know that this is one of Mr. Goldwyn's failings, and because they wanted to somehow make a permanent acknowledgment of this endearing fault you are actually going to go outside to witness, ladies and gentlemen, the dedication of the Abe Lastfogel Plaza.

And now, a noted industry leader and philanthropist, the chairman of the board of MCA, who also runs a little antique shop on Adams Boulevard, Mr. Jules Stein.

The next gentleman has produced one major motion picture after another. In honor of his latest, he has come here today with a list of one-syllable words and phrases which were *cut* from *Who's Afraid of Virginia Woolf?*

The list will be recited for you a bit later by Irene Dunne.

But this man is one of the true pioneers in the production, distribution and exhibition of motion pictures; one of the pioneers in the development of talking pictures. As a matter of fact he is one of the pioneers in the development of *talking* itself, having nothing to do with pictures.

Ladies and gentlemen, the president of Warner Brothers Pictures, Inc., Mr. Jack L. Warner.

Mr. Jack Lemmon remarked earlier that Mr. Goldwyn has always been very generous with people less fortunate than himself. And that's really something, too, when you realize that *everybody* is less fortunate than Sam Goldwyn.

(*Looking at card*) Next, a wonderful human being who really —oh, that's *me*.

Next, a man who has been for many years a distinguished industry leader. He is also chairman of the board of the Association of Motion Pictures and Television Producers, Inc. Ladies and gentlemen, one of the great *questions* of our time: Y. Frank Freeman?

According to the next card in my hand I was to have introduced Mr. Richard D. Zanuck. Mr. Zanuck, unfortunately, is not here. Come to think of it, some of the biggest names in our industry are not here today. I'm sure Mr. Goldwyn is very touched by that fact.

Will Rogers, you know, started out as a cowboy and ended up as a comedian. Here is a man who started out in pictures as a comedian and is ending up as a cowboy. One of our all-time great stars, Mr. James Stewart.

(*After Stewart spoke*) You know, I never listen to James Stewart or Jimmy Cagney speak that they don't sound to me like an *impression*.

We're going to try to get this over with as fast as possible because of the tremendous heat out here. While I am speaking to you, these ladies in the blue uniforms will pass among you handing out salt tablets.

WOMAN IN CROWD: "We're not nurses, we're volunteers."

ALLEN: "Then meet me in the parking lot."

Next, ladies and gentlemen, the secretary-treasurer of the Studio Transportation Drivers Union, Local 399, and you'd better give him a big hand because he may be the only man here who knows for sure how to get back into town—Mr. Ralph H. Clare.

The next gentleman is executive vice-president of the Society of Independent Producers. Personally, I have always thought that producers are too independent as it is. Nevertheless, here is Mr. Eugene Arnstein.

Now a gentleman who, despite his imposing record, has frankly accomplished very little since I introduced him about forty-five minutes ago. Mr. George Bagnall.

REMARKS AT BENEFIT FOR WESTMINISTER COMMUNITY CENTER, AT IT'S BOSS IN HOLLYWOOD (JUNE 26, 1966)

Welcome to Watts West.

Perhaps it's a sign that I'm getting old, but I must say that I am conditioned to appreciate old-fashioned names for night clubs. Names like Copacabana, Trocadero, The Cocoanut Grove. I really don't understand this new trend toward giving night clubs names such as It's Boss.

I understand they are opening a new place across the street called It's Dumb.

And there's a place up in the next block called It's Something Else. I went into it last night and it *is* something else. It's a Chinese laundry.

And the names of vocal quartets these days are beyond my understanding too. In my day singing groups had names that were entirely appropriate. The Pied Pipers, The Modernaires, The Melodears. You had only to hear such names to know they designated a vocal group. Today the names of musical groups are ridiculous. I want you people sitting near to the back of the room to turn around and look at the bulletin that gives the names of attractions coming to this club, so you won't think I'm making this up. You see who is booked in here next week? The Leaves.

And look who is following them in the following week: The Moonrakers.

I guess they are going to rake the leaves.

FRAGMENTS FROM ADDRESS AT NBC AWARD LUNCHEON
(DECEMBER 2, 1966)

(At the time of this affair Allen was working on the ninety-minute "Tonight Show" three evenings a week, as well as doing his Sunday evening program.)

Good afternoon, gentlemen. I consider it a great honor to be asked to speak at this gathering, the purpose of which is to honor the men who have been with RCA for a quarter of a century. I not only consider it an honor, I also think it somewhat fitting that I was invited here because as a result of the schedule NBC has me on, I believe I have done the equivalent of twenty-five years of work in the last eight weeks.

First of all, let me announce that Mr. Sarnoff is sorry he could not be here in person today. Mr. Sacks is also sorry that he is not here. And Mr. Weaver is sorry that Mr. Trammell *is* here.

Looking down the list of names on the program I can certainly see a great many whose personal stories are intertwined with the history of NBC. Just to pick a few at random here, I see first the name of Ed Cullen. Ed started with this firm many years ago as a ham operator. I believe prior to his joining the company he had been employed by Armour & Company in the same capacity.

REMARKS TO THE SOCIETY OF MOTION PICTURE AND TELEVISION
ENGINEERS

On Monday, April 30, 1951, about a thousand members of the Society of Motion Picture and Television Engineers gathered for the Society's sixty-ninth semiannual convention. New York's Statler Hotel was chosen by the membership as a location for the get-together. At nine-thirty in the morning registration activities got underway in the foyer of the Georgian Room, followed by an advance sale of luncheon and banquet tickets. At twelve-thirty the members drifted into the Georgian Room proper and seated themselves for lunch. At about twelve forty-five Mr. Allen, checking over the printed schedule, was unnerved to note that his appearance was advertised as a "Topical Address by an Eminent Speaker."

Glancing further down the page he saw that Monday afternoon had been set aside for a "Film and Processing Session," that at 3:00 P.M. Henry Hood, committee chairman, would introduce the "16- and 8-Mm Motion Picture Committee Report," that there would shortly follow a demonstration by F. L. Bray of Du-Art Film Laboratories, Inc., of "A New Processing Machine Film Spool for Use With Either 35-Mm or 16-Mm Film," and that this demonstration would in turn be followed by a discussion of "Experiments in High Speed Processing Using Turbulent Fluids."

Feeling that the usual recital of postluncheon jokes would be out of place, Allen made a few hasty notes on the back of his program, ate his meal on a nervous stomach, was introduced, rose and made substantially the following remarks:

Good afternoon. You may notice that in your schedule pamphlet you were promised a topical address by an eminent speaker. I am speaking to you today. Obviously something has gone wrong.

Actually, I have nothing prepared for you this afternoon in the way of a formal speech, because I didn't realize I was going to be called upon till about twelve weeks ago, but before I do say what I have to say I must make an announcement or two. First of all, the management of the Statler Hotel has asked me to tell you how sorry the Statler is about the crowded conditions that existed in the rest rooms before you all came into the ballroom. More people showed up for this luncheon than had been expected evidently, and things were pretty uncomfortable out there in the foyer. Anyway, the management is very sorry, and they want me to tell you that *after* this meeting breaks up . . . it's going to happen again.

This time, however, they're prepared, and they have made it

possible for you to use the rest rooms at the parking lot across the street.

Now, in looking over your schedule of activities here I've come across a few things that I think deserve to be brought to your attention because it's quite possible that you won't get to attend each and every lecture on the schedule.

This afternoon, for example, at three forty-five, Elmore Dunsmuir, known to you all I'm sure, will offer a fascinating report on "New Methods of High Speed Processing Using Battery Acid in a Flit Gun."

Then tomorrow morning in Room 1409, Roger Price, Columbia's consultant on color television, will discuss at nine-thirty the project to which he is currently devoting the great part of his time: "Color Radio."

Thursday morning a special treat has been planned, for that's the morning that George Fangschleister will be here. George, as you probably don't need to be told, was the man who way back in 1924, while trying to invent a new developing fluid, took a mixture of ice, citric acid, potassium and gin, shook it up in a metal cylinder and discovered that by some miscalculation he had invented the martini.

Thursday afternoon will bring one of the high spots of the convention, and I don't suppose any of you who heard the talk last year by Jerome Fern will argue with me on that score. Jerome is going to give us the over-all picture in color television, a discussion of over-all factors in kinescope recording, and an over-all idea of developments in the three-dimensional movie field. As you old-timers will recall, Jerome works in Flint, Michigan, for the Oshkosh Overall people, and though he doesn't know beans about photography he nevertheless is adept at giving us the over-all picture.

Then Thursday afternoon, more good news! Abner Sylvester will be on hand to discuss the sensational new Sylvester lens. This is the lens which is so good that it doesn't even require a camera, and I know that you'll all want to ask Mr. Sylvester a great many questions about it.

Friday afternoon it'll be down to business again as we hear

Henry Hood, your vice-president, in an address of timely significance to the industry, "Thomas Edison and the Recall of General MacArthur."

Following this there will be an open forum to discuss the most serious problem that faces the industry today: the *film shortage*. Heading up this meeting will be Arthur K. Frubweather, of the Pepsodent Company, who will run off an illuminating short subject titled "How We Get Film From Teeth."

In closing, I'd like to say that it was a wonderful treat to again address you members of the Kiwanis, and I think you're to be congratulated for the magnificent work you're doing. I don't know just what it is but you must be doing something. You couldn't have just come here to eat.

Thank you again, and good day.

REMARKS AT THE LOTUS CLUB

(In 1955, shortly before his book *Bop Fables* was published, Simon & Schuster asked Allen to address a group of booksellers at a breakfast meeting in the Lotus Club of New York. Since it was a small and informal gathering Allen allowed himself, while speaking, to be prompted from time to time by the late Jack Goodman of Simon & Schuster, with the following results.)

Ladies and gentlemen, I actually have nothing in particular in mind to say to you this morning. I don't know about the rest of you but I came here to eat.

Of course, I *am* interested in books. That is to say, I have been reading them for a great many years. I firmly believe that when it comes to reading there is nothing like a book. I also feel that I shouldn't speak too long now or in any way delay the accomplishment of the purposes for which we are here gathered, whatever they may be.

If any.

Now then, what would you like me to talk about?

(Jack Goodman shouted, "Mention the records!")

Oh, yes. The records.

Well, first of all they are round. One thing I must admit, how-ever; they *do* have a hole in the middle, but this can easily be plugged up. The records, incidentally, have the same name as the book which Simon & Schuster is about to publish: *Bop Fables*.

As a matter of fact, I was asked to write the book as a result of the success of the recordings. I did fear for a time that the book might suffer precisely *because* the records had sold so well; I feared the record buyers were the same as book buyers, but I am now of the opinion that the reverse is the case, although I'm not sure what the reverse is.

Oddly enough, although bop lingo is something of a fad, there have been no indications that the fad is dying out. It has been running now for about four years. Evidently there is still money to be made from it.

(At this point Goodman said: "Tell them about your jacket," as he pointed to a large 3- by 5-foot projection of the book's cover on a nearby screen.)

Oh, yes. Well, my jacket is a herringbone tweed in a three-but-ton model . . .

(Goodman shouted: "No, no! I meant the book jacket!")

Oh. Well, to begin with, I had no idea it was so *big*. I imagine a book this large will cause a great deal of confusion among booksellers; although now that I think of it this is not the first big book that Simon & Schuster has published. Just the other day Mr. Goodman presented me with a copy of an exceedingly heavy volume entitled *American Science and Invention*. It is a fine book but it is quite heavy. As a matter of fact, you buy it by the pound. I found it much too weighty to hold in my hands, and had to read it kneeling on the floor.

(At this point memory fails. Allen spoke for some twenty min-utes, but since his remarks were extemporaneous he has no further recollection as to what transpired.)

REMARKS AT THE AMERICAN PSYCHIATRIC ASSOCIATION MEETING
(OCTOBER 5–8, 1972)

I'm sorry that Jayne and I were a bit late driving in this morning. I was trying to hurry along on Shell of the Future; unfortunately we've got a car of the past.

Incidentally, if Dr. Henry Mortensen of Des Moines, Iowa, is in the audience, and if he's the same Henry Mortensen who twenty-one years ago left his wife and baby in Des Moines, Iowa, I have been instructed to tell Dr. Mortensen that if he will step out into the parking lot, the baby will kick the hell out of him.

A number of fascinating addresses have been—or will be—delivered at this convention.

My attention was drawn particularly to Doctor Kenneth Cohen's paper titled "The Psychiatrist in the General Hospital: How Can He Get Out?"

Those of you who are familiar with Dr. Cohen's views will already know that he argues that "Progressive investment in technology interferes with the physician's capacity to relate to his patient."

Actually, what Dr. Cohen *means* to say here is "Progressive *involvement* in technology."

As a matter of fact, *investment* in technology, in the form of stocks in IBM, North-American Rockwell, etc., has greatly improved Dr. Cohen's own financial position, as a result of which he finds it easier to relate not only to his patients, but to everyone.

Except to his brother Irving, who touted him off Polaroid.

We also look forward to hearing a rendering of Dr. Gordon Jensen's paper titled "College Manpower for the Mental Health Advancement of Teen-agers and Youth."

As those of you familiar with Dr. Jensen may already be aware, he has some remarkable views on the subject of child psychiatry.

36

He believes, for example, that the real meaning of the phrase "child psychiatrist" is that we should enable a number of small children to become psychiatrists.

Dr. Jensen also places great emphasis, as you may know, on peer counseling groups. He is, in fact, one of the chief experts in the field of peer counseling.

Some of you may be personally familiar with the wonderful work he has done on the piers in San Diego, San Pedro and other port cities on the West Coast.

Laugh if you will, but many a once-disturbed longshoreman owes his present peace of mind to Dr. Jensen. And if that isn't pier counseling, I don't know what is.

I have also been very impressed—as I have studied the pamphlet including the abstracts of a number of important convention addresses—by the fine work being done by Dr. Richard Rahe, of San Diego.

In this connection I am reminded—and this happens to be a true story—of a visit that Jayne and I made a few years ago to the Naval Hospital in San Diego, where we did what little we could to try to cheer up some injured servicemen, most of whom had recently come back from Vietnam.

For some reason, when making hospital visits of this sort, it often happens that the visitor asks the injured man where he was when he was wounded.

In bed after bed, young sailors and marines told me they were just outside this or that village, in a truck convoy, in a helicopter or whatever.

Finally I turned to a husky-looking young man who appeared to be Mexican-American.

After making what I hoped was some cheerful small talk, I said, "And where were you injured?"

"I was hit by a Volkswagen in San Diego," he explained.

We're also honored to have a marvelous doctor, Morton Feldman, who has recently made a series of statistical studies to determine why his men patients get up at night.

37

Some of you may be familiar with his findings, which are that 11 per cent get up to go to the icebox, 27 per cent get up to go to the bathroom.

And 9 per cent get up to go home.

Another advertised address that we won't be able to hear, unfortunately, is the one to have been delivered by a Dr. William Gorney who—as you may know—has done heroic work in the field of censorship and pornography.

Dr. Gorney had hoped to deliver his brilliant paper tomorrow morning on the subject of the psychiatric implications of X-rated movies.

Unfortunately, the convention authorities, having previewed Dr. Gorney's paper, considered that it was too vulgar to read publicly.

Dr. Thomas A. Sturgis will be speaking on how to deal with baldness in women and—more importantly—how to tell bald women from bald men.

At two o'clock tomorrow we will hear about "Diagnosis and Management of Breakdown" by Ralph Walderstein. At two-thirty we will hear a talk titled "Breakdown and Diagnosis of Management," also by Dr. Walderstein.

Later in the afternoon Dr. Ernest Butler will lecture on the dangerous side effects of antihistamine and the dangerous side effects of *pro*histamine.

Dr. Butler, you know, was the first one to preserve the human brain in alcohol, with a dash of vermouth.

Although he is perhaps best-known for having combined methadrin and anahist to make a new cold remedy called "Methodist."

Unfortunately, two gentlemen who had originally planned to be with us during the convention will not be able to appear. One is Dr. Sorensen, who is suffering from Huntington's disease.

And Dr. Huntington, who is suffering from Sorensen's disease.

Another eminent medical figure will be absent. George Abramson, who as you know has done remarkable work in the field of Huntington's chorea, through some sort of mistake has this week gone directly to Panmunjom, to continue his Korean studies.

Incidentally, an unscheduled address has been added to the program and will be delivered personally by Dr. Goldzband himself. The title of his talk is "Our Convention: Should It Have Been Held in Miami?"

I would say that the one dominant reaction I have had, after having read the abstracts of every major address to be presented here in the next four days, is that I personally experience every single symptom referred to.

Chapter Two

STEVE ALLEN: AD LIB

The question is put to Steve Allen, "Do you believe in reincarnation? If so, what would you like to come back as?" Steve answers, "I'd like to come back as fast as I can."
back with an ad lib as fast.

On Steve's twenty-fifth anniversary program his friend Jack Carter complained. "You had to blow your whole life on this stupid evening," he lamented. "There's no food, no tables, and a rented audience." In responding, Steve, usually so articulate, blew a line. He said, "Twenty-five years ago, perhaps for having committed serious offenses in radio, I was sentenced to twenty-five years in television. I have now served that sentence with *no at off* . . ." Steve quickly corrected himself, "with no *time* at all off for good behavior." Then instantly added, "or for good diction." A fast mind.

With Allen, ad libs come not only fast and furiously but effortlessly. Spiritualist Kenny Kingston claimed that with his special powers he had seen the deceased Humphrey Bogart and Mayor Jimmy Walker the night before at the Sahara Hotel. Steve's re-
One thing is certain, and that is there are few who can come

sponse: "I didn't know that when you die you go to the Sahara Hotel."

On another occasion Countess Luciana Pignatelli was on Steve's show to promote a book on beauty. On the book's cover there appeared the phrase "As told to Jeanne Molli." Steve equipped: "Well, it only goes to prove what I've always said—that Jeanne Molli is a notorious blabbermouth. You tell her something, she writes a book."

If women gave birth to babies at the rate Allen gives birth to ad libs, our planet would be doomed by overpopulation. There are men of letters who feel, however, that our world is already overpopulated with shallow ad libs. Literary critics usually rate ad libs and puns low on the comic scale, arguing that the witticisms of Groucho Marx or a Robert Benchley pale compared to the more profound humorous observations of an Oscar Wilde or George Bernard Shaw. Such comparison misses the whole point of the ad lib.

If these literary critics knew their horse operas as well as they know opera, they would realize that what counts in the showdown is one man's ability to face the other. In *The Lawman*, Burt Lancaster explained to a gun fighter he might be coming up against, "You might be faster, but I could kill you." Even in the "B" Western, human confrontation is what counts. It is also what matters in ad libbing. In the tumult of everyday life what's required is not a power to chisel eternal truths but simply to get your point across tellingly. That the ad lib does. In the daily war of words it is a trusty weapon. The significance of the ad lib doesn't consist in its profundity, but in its capacity to work for the individual under fire. Economist J. M. Keynes observes that in the long run you're dead. Thus what happens in the short run is highly important. Truly profound utterances are infrequent. Things would get rather dull if we had nothing to say while waiting for great pearls of wisdom. The witty ad lib serves the art of conversation richly.

In his discussion of Milton Berle in *The Funny Men*, Steve Allen graphically etched the point. He concedes that Berle's material may not sound impressive when read in cold print. Yet because he is such a consummate performer it is different when Berle is in action. Allen correctly observes that Berle—like Don Rickles or Jack Carter—would defeat the wittiest humorists in actual combat. He recalls the fate of the clever Henry Morgan one night when he tried to cross comic swords with Milton. "With insults, old jokes, new jokes, mugging, voice volume, arm waving, interrupting and every trick in the trade, Milton succeeded in making Henry look like an inept newcomer."

The great ad libber, such as Allen, doesn't work on paper but in life. One night on the Merv Griffin show actor Gavin Mac-Leod mentioned that he was a Pisces, which is the water sign. Later in the show MacLeod complained that his part on "McHale's Navy" had not been right for him. Allen inquired, "You didn't think 'McHale's Navy' was a good place for a Pisces?"

While guest-hosting the Merv Griffin show Steve said, "If my mind ever listened to what my mouth said, I'd have a lot of accounting to do."

Obviously his mouth invariably listens to what his mind is saying, because his ad libs make remarkable sense. It is even more important that his mouth listens to his heart; the power his capacity for ad libbing gives him is always exercised with feeling for his fellow man. Allen once stated, "I don't say half the funny things that pop into my head for fear I'll hurt someone's feelings."

THE BIRTH OF "THE TONIGHT SHOW"

Steve Allen did not begin his ad-libbing career on the NBC late-night program (eventually called "Tonight") in 1954–55–56 that set the style for all subsequent versions of the show by Jack Paar, Johnny Carson, Merv Griffin, David Frost, Dick Cavett and Mike Douglas. The basic ingredient of the program, Allen working with his studio audience, was actually introduced much earlier in his career. It was on a late-night radio show in Los Angeles in 1948–49–50 that he developed the type of free-wheeling comedy interviews, totally ad lib, that now seems to characterize his style.

Fortunately one recording from this series remains. The following pages are a partial transcript of it. Allen had selected four women from his studio audience, brought them onstage, seated them in chairs and—as the program went on the air—prepared to interview them. As he began to speak, one of the ladies onstage happened to idly pick up the wire that dangled from his microphone, at which cue Allen opened the program with what is actually an old joke. From that point on, however, what happened was freshly minted, unplanned, chaotic, absurd, original and typically Allen. (*An asterisk indicates where audience laughter occurred.*)

ALLEN: Handle this wire carefully on the end. See, this part of it right here? Touch that, please.

LADY: Touch it?

ALLEN: Yes. Do you feel anything?

LADY: Not a thing.

ALLEN: Well, don't touch the other end, there's ten thousand volts in it. (*)

By the way, who is your next of kin, in case anything comes up again?

LADY: My husband.

ALLEN: And who's next to him? (*) Who are you?

LADY: Mrs. Lawrence Wren.

ALLEN: Wren? I'm glad you were able to fly in tonight. (*)

Somebody has put on the stage here a bottle of Dad's Old-fashioned Root Beer. They've neglected to include an opener. Oh, do you have one? A fellow just threw up his keys, with an opener attached. How're you going to get home tonight, Mac? (*) Who *are* you, by the way?

ANSWER: Brooks Covell.

ALLEN: Brooks Covell? I used to buy clothing there quite often. Is this from you, too, Brooks, this Dad's Old-Fashioned Root Beer? No? Then who *is* it from?

Maybe my *dad* is here, I don't know. He's just old-fashioned enough to give me root beer. (*)

You know, this really hits the spot. And my spot hasn't been hit for quite awhile. (*)

44

Now, I'll go over and talk to our contestants. One of them I've already had the pleasure of meeting: Mrs. Wren. What does *Mr.* Wren do?

MRS. WREN: He's unemployed at the present.

ALLEN: What about his past?

MRS. WREN: He worked for Gates' Rubber factory in Denver, Colorado.

ALLEN: Well, I can see why he's unemployed. I don't imagine there's much of a market for rubber gates. (*)

I mean, if you come home loaded, you'll fall right through them. (*)

What is he looking for out here?

MRS. WREN: He just came here on a pleasure trip.

ALLEN: Has it been pleasurable?

MRS. WREN: Very much so.

ALLEN: What are you doing for amusement, besides going to radio shows?

MRS. WREN: Just taking in the sights.

ALLEN: Stop looking at *me* like that, will you? (*) What *other* sights have you seen?

MRS. WREN: We've been to 'Frisco, Reno and all down the coast.

ALLEN: 'Frisco and Reno where you played Bingo and Screeno. What did you do at Reno?

MRS. WREN: We saw Harold's Club.

ALLEN: Did Harold hit you with it? (*) How much did you drop?

MRS. WREN: Well, I wouldn't like my friends to know.

ALLEN: If they'd stop seeing you on that account, they're not very good friends.

We're going to play a recording in a few minutes, Mrs. Wren, and if you can tell me the names of the people who are singing on the record you'll be the winner. I forgot what the record is, but we'll all hear it at the same time and start off even. That's the way we play the game; as soon as you know who the singers are put up your hand. And if you are first with the correct answer, you are

45

immediately thrown out of the studio. (*) Because we don't have any decent prizes for you. But if you all lose, then we have some nice *consolation* prizes. (*) Believe me, these prizes are small consolation, (*) but there are some very nice things—such as an empty bottle of Dad's Old-Fashioned Root Beer; (*) and a four years' supply of quick-frozen thyroid extract. (*) One thing we may be able to dispense tonight, out of our beneficence, whatever that means, is some Lady Marlowe Cream Fluff Shampoo. Have you tried it?

MRS. WREN: No, I haven't.

ALLEN: What *have* you tried? Johnson's Wax? (*) What do you ordinarily use to shampoo your hair? I want you to speak frankly.

MRS. WREN: Just plain soap.

ALLEN: And how *long* have you been playin' with this soap? (*) No, what do you prefer, Fels-Naptha and steel wool, or (*) do you have your own little mixture?

MRS. WREN: I usually have my hair done at the beauty shop.

ALLEN: You don't pay much attention to what they use?

MRS. WREN: Some oil; I don't know what the name of it is.

ALLEN: Probably Standard, 30-Weight. (*) Well, this is Lady Marlowe Cream Fluff Shampoo, in case things are ever tough and you can't get to the beauty parlor. Personally, I think more women *should* go to beauty parlors. The Lady Marlowe people aren't going to enjoy hearing me say this, but I think every woman should have her hair done in a beauty parlor. My mother-in-law went to one just last week. She always wears short hair, you know. Looked like a little old woman. Now she looks like a little old man. (*) But it's neat. (*) This is Lady Marlowe Cream Fluff Shampoo. Only thirty-nine cents. For a *barrel* full of it.

Hold up that hogshead over there, will you? (*) Nothing *personal*, Don. (*) You know. I've never smelled Lady Marlowe's Cream Fluff Shampoo. (*) Say, I know what I'll have to do; I'll have to take this home and use it in the smell test. That's a thing we do at our house all the time. We have people in and after we've shown them the slides and the family albums and played the records, then finally someone says, "Well, what'll we do? Does anybody want to play charades?" And somebody else says, "No."

So—what we do at our house: we blindfold people. We get a lot of diapers. (*) What are you laughing at? Clean ones, naturally. (*) They make very nice blindfolds. They go three times around the head and, with a roll of Scotch tape, you can't see a thing. (*) We get about twenty-five common objects—from the medicine cabinet, from the refrigerator, the food chest . . . and you'd be surprised, when blindfolded, how few familiar household objects—the foods you eat, the things you rub on your hair and so forth—how few of them you can identify. As a matter of fact, if you use about twenty-five objects, you're doing very well if you can correctly identify ten of them.

Now this has a unique odor; it doesn't smell anything like shampoo. What would *you* say that smelled like? (*Pause*)

Get up off the floor, quick! (*)

What does it smell like, now that you've come to again?

MRS. WREN: Strawberries.

ALLEN: To me it suggests coconut somehow. What shampoo is it that has coconut milk in it, do you know?

MRS. WREN: Fitch's.

ALLEN: Fitch's has coconut *oil* but this actually smells like coconut milk. Coconut milk, that's silly. You'd have to have a mighty high *stool*, to milk a coconut. (*) Well, Mrs. Coconut Milk . . . er, Mrs. *Wren*, I'm going to jump over here now and find out who contestant number two is, if I may.

And what is your name?

MRS. MICHAEL: Mrs. Michael.

ALLEN: What do you do?

MRS. MICHAEL: I'm with Luzier's, Inc., Cosmetics, in Kansas City, Missouri.

ALLEN: Whom, Inc.?

MRS. MICHAEL: Luzier's. (*Loose ears*)

ALLEN: And how long have you been troubled by this looseness in the ears? (*)

47

MRS. MICHAEL: Six years.

ALLEN: Have you tried Scotch tape? (*)

MRS. MICHAEL: Yes, I have.

ALLEN: What are you doing for amusement?

MRS. MICHAEL: Oh, we're going to broadcasts, the theatre, we saw *The Thief of Bagdad*, eating in some nice places.

ALLEN: You saw *The Thief of Bagdad* eating in some nice places? (*) Well, it's a crazy town. What about Hollywood, has it disappointed you?

MRS. MICHAEL: I just arrived in Hollywood proper today.

ALLEN: How did you come out here—improperly? (*)

MRS. MICHAEL: Very properly.

ALLEN: Are you a driver?

MRS. MICHAEL: I do drive, but not here, though.

ALLEN: Chicken? (*)

MRS. MICHAEL: I'm afraid so.

ALLEN: That's all right. You see chickens driving better than people out here. (*) Well, it was nice meeting you, Mrs. Michael. Now I'll sneak over here and meet the lady in black, the woman of mystery. Who *are* you?

LADY: Yvonne Kenwood, now living in Altadena.

ALLEN: Where were you from, previously?

MRS. KENWOOD: I've been abroad for the past eight years.

ALLEN: A broad, huh? (*) You folks noticed when that happened I was just sitting here? (*) Where were you?

MRS. KENWOOD: All over England.

ALLEN: Are you an entertainer?

MRS. KENWOOD: No, I'm not.

ALLEN: A *spy*? (*)

MRS. KENWOOD: Nothing as exciting.

ALLEN: What do you do?

MRS. KENWOOD: Well, actually, I'm an animal welfare worker. (*)

ALLEN: You look human to me. (*)

No, you're actually very pretty. I'm saying that so the folks at home can get some sort of a picture here. (*) And I'll have it developed in the morning. (*) Where did you buy that unusual hat?

MRS. KENWOOD: In England.

ALLEN: Is this a complete ensemble?

MRS. KENWOOD: Oh, yes.

ALLEN: Would you describe it to the ladies listening? I've discovered, through the mail . . . that most of them can't write. (*) I mean that they're interested in what the folks here at the studio are wearing.

MRS. KENWOOD: Well, it's a taffeta dress, full length, with a low neck, and a Gainsborough hat.

ALLEN: And in what borough did you gain that hat?(*)

MRS. KENWOOD: Kent, England.

ALLEN: *Kent*, huh? (*In English accent*) Oh, I suppose you *could* if you *tried*, old girl. (*) But . . . if you kent, then you kent! (*) Carry on! (*) But don't carry on too *much*, of course. (*) Chin up. Nose down! Ears out! Come, come, out from under your chair, my dear. (*) What exactly do you do, Mrs. Kenwood, as an animal husband, or animal welfare worker or whatever?

MRS. KENWOOD: I go on television twice a week and I get a good home for some animal.

ALLEN: Who's that, your producer? (*)

MRS. KENWOOD: No, just a poor dog that might have been found and needs a good home.

ALLEN: That's a producer, all right. (*) But that's wonderful work. How do you turn the trick, when there are so many human beings without homes?

MRS. KENWOOD: Well, there's no such thing as an unwanted dog, but there are such things as unwanted *humans*, believe it or not.

ALLEN: Is Mr. Kenwood with you?

MRS. KENWOOD: No, I'm here with Mr. Wheeler Dryden from the Charles Chaplin Studios, and my daughter. It's her sixteenth birthday.

ALLEN: What is her name?

MRS. KENWOOD: Nana. (*Audience giggles*)

ALLEN: (*To audience*) Don't get sore. (*) It's the woman's daughter, isn't it? Audiences are strange. You folks should have been at the program last night. We had a contest, and played a

49

record by Perry Como. A woman guessed it was Bing Crosby, and everybody groaned as if she were incredibly stupid. They hit the woman, they spit on her, it was awful! (*) All she did was make a little mistake, and those people! How *vicious* they became. (*) Well, your daughter's name is Nana. What is that short for, Banana? (*)

MRS. KENWOOD: Don't say that to *her*.

ALLEN: I didn't; I said it to *you*. (*) My little boy calls bananas "Nanas." (*) Where *are* you, Banana? (*) I mean *Nana?* Oh, how *are* you? She *does* look a little slippery, doesn't she? (*) But she's a very attractive girl. What are her ambitions?

MRS. KENWOOD: Theatrical.

ALLEN: She wants to be an actress. Is she training?

MRS. KENWOOD: She's in training now.

ALLEN: And what is her *fighting* weight? (*) Has she gotten into any pictures?

MRS. KENWOOD: No, but she's been with Mae West in *Diamond Lil,* and Elizabeth Bergner in *Escape Me Never.*

ALLEN: That's fine. Is she interested in radio?

MRS. KENWOOD: Yes, very much.

ALLEN: Would she like to do work in soap operas, such as "Romance in Helen's Tent" and that sort of thing? (*) You may laugh, (in fact, I hear you very distinctly), (*) but radio dramatic shows are a wonderful proving ground for people who later get into breadlines and things. (*) In radio, you know, you have to be able to pick up a script and look at it and say right now, "I can't do this." (*) Whereas in pictures it may take *years* to prove that you're a bum. (*) But a lot of people *have* gone from radio programs to oblivion. (*)

It's station-break time right now. It's twelve-thirty . . . we're in Hollywood . . . we play records. Once a week or so.

Gee, this Dad's Old-Fashioned Root Beer is getting—uh—older all the time. (*) Can't put it down here. Whoops! Piano slants. Sounds like a name for a program. "Carmen Cavallero with 'Piano Slants'." (*) Who are *you?*

LADY: Sue England.

ALLEN: Sue England? That's what we should have done years ago. (*) What do you do, Sue?

MISS ENGLAND: Oh, I do some motion picture acting and modeling.

ALLEN: You do look familiar. Have I seen you on any shirt labels or anything? (*) Oh, *here* you are, on this Dad's Old-Fashioned D.D.T. label. (*) You never know when you're going to run into people, do you? (*) When *were* you run into last? (*)

MISS ENGLAND: (*Laughing*) I don't know how to answer that.

ALLEN: I hardly knew how to *ask* it. (*) And I am sorry that I *did*. Do you model for an agency, Sue?

MISS ENGLAND: No, I model shoes for the manufacturer.

ALLEN: Well, he's wasting the *rest* of you, I'll tell you that. (*) I'm explaining to the folks at home that Miss England is an attractive young lady. She is wearing some very unusual green shoes. She seems to have *three* of them here! (*) Oh, no, your *legs* were crossed; *I* see. (*) Did you design those yourself, or do they grow in your back yard? (*)

MISS ENGLAND: They were given to me by the manufacturer, Mr. Gotts. Well, he isn't really the manufacturer.

ALLEN: He's the delivery boy trying to act big? (*)

MISS ENGLAND: He's the *salesman* for Jay Shoe Company.

ALLEN: What about the dress, where did you get that? The skirt, I mean.

MISS ENGLAND: My fiance gave it to me.

ALLEN: Nuts. (*) How soon?

MISS ENGLAND: How soon am I going to be married?

ALLEN: Make it easy on yourself. (*) Yes.

MISS ENGLAND: In about two years.

ALLEN: And already he's giving you dresses? (*) And the blouse?

MISS ENGLAND: It's all one piece.

ALLEN: Well, I hope it *stays* that way. (*) Those are very pretty shoes. They're a vivid green. What shade of green would you call that?

51

MISS ENGLAND: Kelly.

ALLEN: It looks more like *pool table* to me. (*) It fits very well around the *cue ball*, too. (*) Now, the color of the skirt, what would you call that?

MISS ENGLAND: Well, it's a drab green.

ALLEN: *Grab*, did you say? (*) Oh, *drab*.

MISS ENGLAND: Olive drab.

ALLEN: Well, Ah live pretty drab myself. (*) And what about the blouse?

MISS ENGLAND: That's sort of olive green.

ALLEN: Well, it fits well around the pimento. (*) That's a formula joke. How did you get into the modeling field?

MISS ENGLAND: My friend works for a modeling agency and she let me in on this job, on the sly.

ALLEN: What was the job?

MISS ENGLAND: Modeling shoes.

ALLEN: I thought it was modeling *slys*. (*) This job, you've just started it recently?

MISS ENGLAND: I work off and on. (*)

ALLEN: That's all right. (*) You said you work in pictures. What may we have seen you in?

MISS ENGLAND: In *This Love of Ours*.

ALLEN: Tell me a bit about that. (*)

MISS ENGLAND: Oh, that was too long ago. *City Across the River*.

ALLEN: Oh, yes. Playa del Rey, you mean. (*) What else?

MISS ENGLAND: Oh, *Kidnapped*.

ALLEN: With Roddy McDowall. I saw Roddy last night. They must have paid the ransom, he's out now. (*) What did you do in *Kidnapped*?

MISS ENGLAND: I played the feminine lead.

ALLEN: My goodness! I hope you'll forgive my ignorance. There's always that terrible danger in our business. You meet someone at a party and say, "What do you do?" And he says, "I happen to be George Bernard Shaw!" (*) You meet people at parties and they turn out to be God or somebody. (*) I'm sorry I didn't recognize you. It's only because I didn't see the picture.

MISS ENGLAND: I did some television. Didn't you see that either?

ALLEN: I'm just a big mole, that's all. (*) What show did you do?

MISS ENGLAND: I did the "Lone Ranger." I wasn't the Lone Ranger, though.

ALLEN: Tonto, how are you? (*) I watch the "Lone Ranger" with regularity. That's the name of my oldest boy. (*) Reggie and I sit there every night and watch with gusto. That's my daughter. (*) This is the stupidest program I've ever done in my whole life. (*) What did you do in the "Lone Ranger?"

MISS ENGLAND: I played the governess' daughter who was rescued by the Lone Ranger.

ALLEN: I saw that! You were tremendous! (*) You were lovely. You still are. (*) Who's this fellow you're marrying? Are you sure he's the right one? What does he do?

MISS ENGLAND: He's going to college right now.

ALLEN: What are his plans?

MISS ENGLAND: He's a dancer.

ALLEN: Any plans to *trip*? (*) It's commercial time. What do you use on your hair, Sue?

MISS ENGLAND: Do you really want me to tell you?

ALLEN: I know it won't be what I advertise. (*) But what do you use?

MISS ENGLAND: (*Looks in purse*) I . . . can't . . . find it.

ALLEN: Well, you *can* find it at your Owl Drugstore. Now I happen to have a little of it right here, and it's Wildroot . . . beer. (*) Wait a minute, it's *Wildroot Creme Oil Hair Tonic*.

MISS ENGLAND: That's not what I use. *I use shampoo.*

ALLEN: Oh, I'm sorry. (*) It'd be pretty rough if you used this and expected your hair to get clean, you know? (*) This just gums it up a little, that's all. (*) So does any other oil, so don't get sore if you're listening, Mr. Wildroot. Wildroot Oil Creme, I mean Hair Oil . . . (*) er . . . Wildhair Root Beer, Tonic Creme. Try it, whatever it's called. It's at your Owl Drugstores and they want desperately to get rid of it. (*) They want to get it to you, the customer, so you can put it all over your entire head. No matter what hair tonic you're using today, get Wildroot Creme Oil. I've been drinking it for years because it contains soothing lino-leum, (*) lanolin and not a drop of alcohol. (*) No wonder Wild-root Creme Oil is again and again the choice of men who put to-bacco first. (*) I seem to have my slogans confused. What does it say here? "Wildroot Creme Oil is again and again the choice of men who put good grooming first."

Men in commercials are always putting things first. (*) Smart girls use Wildroot Creme Oil, too, it says here—for training chil-dren's hair. Now what can you train your child's hair to do? A cartwheel? (*) Just offer his scalp some Creme Oil, and don't give it to him until it does those *tricks*. (*) That's the first thing you learn about training anything. Did you ever *train* any dog, Mrs. Kenwood.

MRS. KENWOOD: Well, a soldier presented me with Her-mann Goering's own personal police dog and I had to detrain him myself because he was very vicious. He was a guard at Bal-four and now he's exceptionally gentle.

ALLEN: Fascinating story. How long did it take you?

MRS. KENWOOD: About four months.

ALLEN: What sort of dog is he?

MRS. KENWOOD: He's a very handsome German Shepherd, the largest in the world.

ALLEN: What's his name?

MRS. KENWOOD: Baron von Zeiglehoff.

ALLEN: Is there a radio in his hut? (*) Think he might be listening? Achtung, baron! (*) And now, hours overdue, it's time for the record! You'll only get to hear three grooves of it and you must give me your answer quickly, and in Latin. (*)

RECORD: "Ashes of Roses"

ALLEN: All right, there it is. Anyone know the singers?

MISS ENGLAND: Ozzie and Harriet Nelson?

ALLEN. No, that happens to be Elton Britt and Rosalie Allen. Well, we again will have to hold our forty-thousand-dollar jack pot (*) over until next week, at which time there'll be no mention of it. (*) As for prizes, we have for each of you some *Hospitality House Bubble Bath.* If you don't have champagne, you can drop a little Hospitality House into some 7-Up and it makes a lovely drink. (*) What else do we have here? Oh, yes. For you, Sue, a one-leg supply of No-Snag, to prevent runs. (*) We have here an old corncob pipe that has been cleverly disguised to look like a revolver. (*) Do you have anybody in the family who smokes, Mrs. Michael?

MRS. MICHAEL: I have a son.

ALLEN: What does he smoke?

MRS. MICHAEL: I wouldn't know.

ALLEN: Haven't you ever smelled it around the house? (*) Does it cause big clouds of smoke?

MRS. MICHAEL: Well, I don't know. It's a pipe similar to that one.

ALLEN: Oh, it is a pipe? Fine. Then here is a pipe for your son. And here's some Lady Marlowe Cream Fluff Shampoo to put in it. (*) Now it's time to hop down into the audience. We have a few minutes or so to meet some folks down in the Snake Pit. (*) Whoops! I hit myself right in the head with the wire. But then who has a better right? (*) Your name, please?

ANSWER: Wayne Barhardt.

ALLEN: What do you do, Wayne?

MR. BARHARDT: I'm a carpenter.

ALLEN: How long have you been carpentering?

MR. BARHARDT: Oh, about sixteen years.

ALLEN: You must be very tired. (*) And who's this with you?

MR. BARHARDT: My wife.

ALLEN: How long have you been married to this carpenter?

MRS. BARHARDT: Thirteen years.

ALLEN: Any little splinters around the house? (*)

MRS. BARHARDT: Two.

ALLEN: Oh, these are *all* Carpenters? Are *you* a carpenter?

SMALL BOY: No.

ALLEN: What *are* you?

SMALL BOY: I don't know. (*)

ALLEN: Well, perhaps I can find out for you. Where did you sleep last night?

SMALL BOY: Home.

ALLEN: When did you see your father last?

SMALL BOY: Thursday.

ALLEN: I don't know what you are, either. (*) I can't worry about everybody's problems, you know. (*) Miss Kenwood, don't go away, I may have something for the *baron* here! (*) What is your name, sir?

ANSWER: Ed Nelson.

ALLEN: What do you do, Ed?

MR. NELSON: I am employed by the government.

ALLEN: In what capacity?

MR. NELSON: The Navy.

ALLEN: Are these all your friends here?

MR. KROGER: No, we don't know them.

ALLEN: Well, give them a chance, will you? (*) You fellows from the East?

ANSWER: That's right.

ALLEN: I thought perhaps by the jackets that you might be. Where are you from?

ANSWER: Massachusetts.

ALLEN: Where do you go to school back there?

ANSWER: Upsala College.

ALLEN: Watch your language. (*) What are you studying for?

ANSWER: I'm an English major.

ALLEN: Are you studying to teach English or to speak it?

ANSWER: To speak it.

ALLEN: Good luck, you're getting close. (*) What's your name, in case your friends are listening? We actually get mail from Massachusetts.

ANSWER: (*Loudly*) Roy Peterson.

ALLEN: Sounds like you're calling him. (*) If you're out there, Roy! (*) Oh, *you're* Roy Peterson. And who are you?

ANSWER: Ken Hedlin.

ALLEN: Do you fellows hear programs like this in Massachusetts?

ANSWER: Not often.

ALLEN: They know what they're doing back there, believe me.

(*) A gentleman just took his glasses off to wipe his eyes. Who are you?

ANSWER: Herbert Trednick.

ALLEN: What do you do, Herb?

MR. TREDNICK: I'm a student.

ALLEN: What are you studying?

MR. TREDNICK: Psychology.

ALLEN: Must you look at *me* like that? (*) You here on business or pleasure, Herb?

MR. TREDNICK: I don't know, to tell you the truth.

ALLEN: Have you become acquainted at all with audience or mob psychology?

MR. TREDNICK: Not so far.

ALLEN: I keep looking for people who are interested in that because I am. This other lady with the sober expression?

ANSWER: I'm a social worker.

ALLEN: Well, let's be a little more sociable, then. (*) Are you working with Herb?

ANSWER: No.

ALLEN: Do you know Herb?

ANSWER: Oh, somewhat.

ALLEN: You aren't his wife, are you?

ANSWER: No.

ALLEN: Where is his wife? (*)

ANSWER: Ohhh, she's in . . . er—

ALLEN: That'll do, that'll do! (*) You work socially through what agency?

ANSWER: I'm unemployed now.

ALLEN: You'll help anybody, huh? (*) Somebody back there has a familiar laugh. Stick a rag in his mouth. (*) Now, who are you, sir?

ANSWER: Bill Oliver.

ALLEN: Were you in here once before?

MR. OLIVER: No.

ALLEN: I thought not. I knew you'd never have the nerve to come back. (*) Is this Mrs. Oliver?

MR. OLIVER: Yes.

ALLEN: How long have you been married, Mrs. Oliver?

MRS. OLIVER: (*Quietly*) Twenty-three years.

ALLEN: It sounds as if you've hated every minute of it. (*) But it's wonderful to see people married that long and having a lot of fun here together. Do you remember the first time you ever saw Mr. Oliver?

MRS. OLIVER: Yes, I do.

ALLEN: Tell me about it.

MRS. OLIVER: Well . . . it's been so long ago. He came to my home.

ALLEN: Through the window, or what? (*)

MRS. OLIVER: No, he walked in the front door. Someone had told him to come over to my house to see me. So he did. That's all.

ALLEN: Gee, it was easy in those days, wasn't it? (*) I've walked into thousands of girls' homes but only married one. (*) Mrs. Oliver, which one of you listens and dragged the other one in?

MR. OLIVER: We both have been very interested in your program.

ALLEN: Interested? (*) Somehow that word hurts a little. (*) You mean you've laughed at it?

MR. OLIVER: Well, we've listened to you over the radio and we finally decided to come up here and see what you look like. (*)

ALLEN: I notice that you're no longer smiling. (*) You're laughing right out loud. (*) Well, it's nice of you to come in. Time's up and I can't think of anything else to add. Anything I'm forgetting to say? I often go off the air and head for home, and suddenly I say, "Son-of-a-gun, I forgot to mention so-and-so." So if you're listening tonight, so-and-so, remember I mentioned you. (*) You were a nice audience; give yourselves a round of applause.

THE OWL PEOPLE AND OTHER CREATURES OF THE NIGHT

It has frequently been remarked that Allen has the disconcerting habit of chuckling in the middle of a conversation, sometimes for no apparent reason. There *is* a reason, of course, Steve explains, "but it does not become apparent because I have no desire to derail most conversations. What I am laughing at is usually a double meaning that has suddenly occurred to me. Sometimes, of course—particularly when I am on the air—I *do* stop the conversation and make capital of the digression. For example, years ago I was sponsored by the Owl Drugstores, in Hollywood. One night I picked up a commercial that started "Friends, the Owl people are bringing you this program—" and I broke up because the phrase "Owl people" suddenly suggested to me a weird race of creatures from another planet, all covered with feathers, having great staring eyes and big claws. Far off in a corner of my mind I could hear an insane voice shouting, "Better run, Captain Jack. Here come the Owl people!" To this day I smile when I pass an Owl Drugstore.

The bespectacled comic's tendency to play with double meanings (though *not* in an off-color way) is evident in the following ad-lib interview, of which there is a transcript because it was recorded—in 1949—by a company called Radio Reports.

ALLEN: Is Elson Irwin in the audience tonight? Are you Elson Irwin? I'm so glad you showed up tonight. I never needed you more. Who are you?

No, I know who you are. I'm just kidding, Mr. Irwin.

You may recall that about two months ago, Margaret Whiting and Steve Allen were named the big nothings of National Tea Week.

I was selected as the person who best exemplified the ability to work under pressure and I had my picture taken, and it was reported, by means of a caption wherever the picture was reproduced, that when under pressure I would cool off with a tall glass of iced tea. In the interest of honesty, however, I reported that what was actually in the glass when they took the pictures was Coca-Cola. The reason they used Coca-Cola is because it's very easy to get Coca-Cola in the middle of the day. You just put a nickel in a machine and you have Coca-Cola, but you can't expect a photographer to walk around with a musette bag full of hot water and a bunch of tea bags.

So we had a glass full of ice cubes and Coke with lemon and straws to make it look like iced tea. In fact, it photographed more like iced tea than iced tea does. It developed that iced tea photographs like Drano.

So again I say, in the interest of honesty, I simply reported that development, and I also admitted that when I am really under pressure and want to cool off, I drink *beer*.

Somehow, this all got back to the National Tea Bureau, so I won't be with them next year when thirst-quenching time rolls around.

But they reported that story to a gentleman named Red Doff (who is my publicity man) and I saw the photostatic copies of the protest. You would have thought I was going to be deported from the country. They had it all down in black and white against me (or white and black, I should say; they were photostats).

It seems there is an organization called Radio Reports, Incorporated, and these are the people who ratted on me.

But they do that for a living and it's perfectly all right. When I heard about them and found out that I couldn't do anything to them, I was so intrigued that I invited one of the members of their organization down here tonight and that is Elson Irwin, to whom we were just speaking.

As long as I've nothing else planned for the next couple of minutes, Mr. Irwin, I'd like to ask you a few questions. Exactly what is Radio Reports, Incorporated?

IRWIN: Well, you might say it's a clipping bureau.

ALLEN: That's what you did to me, all right.

IRWIN: It's the same as a clipping bureau of newspapers, only on radio.

ALLEN: How exactly do you report to one of your clients what went on the radio? Do you send them a record of it? Do you take it down in shorthand?

IRWIN: No. We record it on the air, taking notes while we are recording it, and then send a summary of the program to the client. Then, if he wants it we type it from the record and send it to him as a manuscript.

ALLEN: Oh, *I* must give you a *tremendous* volume of business.

IRWIN: Yes, you do, Steve.

ALLEN: Tell me what you've been doing to me the last month or so.

IRWIN: Well, Steve, it's our business to record every time you mention a brand name on the radio. If it's our client, then they're interested in knowing that you said something about them.

ALLEN: So when are they going to begin sending me all the free things?

It always happens to other people but not to me. I've been mentioning Drano for a long time now.

It'd be nice to have a case of that stuff come in at Christmastime, you know? Just a little token of what they'd like me to swallow.

Tell me more, Elson.

IRWIN: Well, Steve, when you started on radio in the afternoon I was listening to your show and you referred to several products, so I mentioned to our boss that you—

ALLEN: I've been *wondering* why I wasn't on in the afternoon any more!

IRWIN: —that you'd be a good prospect as a program to be listed on our monitoring schedule. So after listening to you for several weeks they decided to take your program as one of our regular shows, and it paid off.

ALLEN: I hope it's done *you* a lot of good. It hasn't meant much to *me*. Who *are* some of your clients, Elson?

IRWIN: Well, I suppose that the main client would be Standard Oil and United States Steel.

ALLEN: Whoever mentions United States Steel on the radio? Nobody gets laughs with United States Steel.

IRWIN: Well, you see, Steve, we don't only record comedians. We also take news broadcasts and commentators.

ALLEN: I wonder what category I fit into?

How did you happen to get with these people, Elson?

IRWIN: I was working for Title Insurance and Trust Company, and then I went to work for Radio Reports. Normally I'm a sports writer. I wrote for the Bakersfield *Press*. I was assistant sports editor up there and then I came down here and went to work for Radio Reports.

ALLEN: And how long have you been down here?

IRWIN: Since last January. This is the second time I've been working for Radio Reports. I worked for them before, before I left for Bakersfield, and now I'm working for them again.

ALLEN: I hope the *third* time it works out. Say, do you know a fellow named Matt Hoffman up there at the Bakersfield paper?

IRWIN: No, I don't.

ALLEN: I don't either.

But if there ever were a fellow by that name, I think he could get a lot of work.

No, seriously, there is. He once wrote a very nice thing about me. It was a death notice or something, but I was very grateful. His name was Matt Hoffman, I believe.

IRWIN: That's the Bakersfield *Californian*. The paper I worked for is not in existence now.

ALLEN: I was wondering why my subscription wasn't coming through.

Well, that's too bad. What was the trouble? Poor circulation, or low blood pressure or—

IRWIN: No. Right after I went to work there, there was a strike.

ALLEN: What were they striking for, greasier newsprint or what?

IRWIN: They were striking for money, I suppose. For money and shorter hours.

ALLEN: Shorter hours? Good. I always did think sixty minutes was too long for an hour.

Well, Elson, I've certainly learned a lot about Radio Reports, although I don't suppose I'll ever learn as much about them as they've learned about me.

What in the world is this here? Mr. Irwin has just whipped out a brochure, a "white paper," which happens to be printed on *pink* paper.

What are these papers here?

IRWIN: Well, Steve, this is an example of a note sheet that we take where we type notes on your program while listening to it and while making a record. These are notes that we take while listening to your program, and they're kind of jumbled but that's—

ALLEN: That's the way the program is, too. Tell me about these notes.

IRWIN: Well, Steve, in front of you here are the notes for every one of your programs for your summer series for Colgate toothpaste.

ALLEN: That was over in a hurry, wasn't it?

IRWIN: Well, in case you want to know what you said, here it is.

ALLEN: I'm trying to *forget* what I said. (*Reads*) "Program analyst's report on Steve Allen replacement for Eve Arden. This analysis is the frank opinion of Elson E. Irwin, who suggested Steve Allen be listed in the regular monitors' schedule when he started a sustaining show over CBS as an afternoon half-hour stripper." There seems to be some mistake here.

"He gave us lots of good material. He consistently mentions trade names, subconsciously and unconsciously."

Listen, *I'm* nobody's fool.

Somebody must want me. "Allen has done so on midnight show over same network of which I have been an avid listener."

How many tubes has your *Avid?*

IRWIN: I don't have an Avid.

ALLEN: "Most of his program consists of very well-written ad libs."

Would you like to revise your estimate on that one point?

Well, Elson, I don't know how to thank you, and there's a good possibility that I won't.

Are these notes of any further use to you?

IRWIN: Well, they go in our files. We keep them for several years and then if nobody wants them we throw them away.

ALLEN: You and I have a date in 1956. Thank you, Elson, for coming up tonight. Anytime you'd like to, drop in.

IRWIN: I'll be glad to, Steve. Steve, I—I—

ALLEN: Come, come. Out with it, man, out with it!

IRWIN: I want to say something, that I thought you had a terrific program.

ALLEN: But?

IRWIN: No, I mean it. Because I look at it from a different standpoint, too. I also have done some entertaining. Not so much on the radio, but on the stage.

ALLEN: Oh, really. What sort of acting are you interested in? (I'll see you folks later).

IRWIN: Not acting, Steve. I was a singer. I did a lot of imitations and so forth.

ALLEN: You do imitations? *I* do imitations. Who do *you* imitate?

IRWIN: I used to do Jolson.

ALLEN: I'll imitate somebody and you imitate somebody. My father can lick your father.

I'd like to imitate one of your movie favorites. Margaret O'Brien. Ah, Benita. If I were king. If I were king, king. If I were *working*.

Now you do one.

IRWIN: Steve, that sounded like Dennis Day's imitation of Ronald Coleman.

ALLEN: It was.

IRWIN: I'm getting away from imitations. They don't pay off. I'd better sing in my own voice.

ALLEN: Don't try to sing in mine.

But would you like to do a little number for us in your own voice? Would you sing something I know, like "Sabre Dance"?

IRWIN: What do you know?

ALLEN: Not much; how's it going? Something old. Let me see. How about "Just A-wearyin' for You"?

IRWIN: I don't know how to sing that.

ALLEN: Yeah, but are you *doing* it? Wearying, I mean.

Well, thanks a lot, Elson. That was very interesting. Elson Irwin, ladies and gentlemen.

64

ANOTHER VIEW OF THE KNX DAYS

(In his novel *Not All of Your Laughter, Not All of Your Tears*, Allen wrote himself into one of the scenes in the open guise of Alan Stevens, late-night gabber. The following section of the novel is based on a more-or-less verbatim transcript of a typical Allen broadcast of the 1949 period.)

Dan controlled himself for the next three days, his unspoken misery mounting. On Thursday evening he met his partner, Hank Lazarus, at the Brown Derby and together they went to station KNX to be interviewed by Al Stevens, the late-night disc jockey and comedian. When they arrived at the CBS Building, a fuzz-cheeked usher showed them to the control room of Studio B. "You can wait right in here," he said. "Mr. Stevens has already started his warmup."

They entered the small, overly air-conditioned cubicle with the slanted plate glass front that overlooked the stage, seated themselves on aluminum and black leatherette chairs, received a curt over-the-shoulder smile from an engineer and looked out at Alan Stevens' back and beyond him at the upturned faces of the studio audience.

"I'd like to take a little survey," Stevens was saying. "Now, let's see. Would those of you who have never been here before please raise your hands?"

About 90 per cent of the people lifted their hands, some innocently, others smirking wisely, suspecting the joke that, knowing Stevens, they felt sure would follow.

"That's fine," he said, seemingly very earnest. "Now may I see the hands of those who are here tonight for the *first time?*"

Most of those who had raised their hands did so again and then slowly the audience started to laugh.

"Funny bit," Hank said.

65

"Yeah," said the engineer, touching a dial. "I've been listening to that same joke every night for the last two years. For some reason every time I see those hands go up the second time I break up."

"We'll be on the air in just a few minutes," Stevens said, pushing a lock of hair off his forehead, "and since this is supposed to be a comedy show I—uh—I suppose I'd better show you some comedy. I mean I suppose you'd better agree to laugh it up. In fact, as an added inducement we have some very nice prizes to give away. For example, the lady who laughs the loudest tonight is going to receive a beautiful five-pound box of wet sand."

"He does the warmup the same every night?" Hank asked.

"Yeah," the engineer said. "The ad libbing starts when we go on the air."

"And we have some other wonderful prizes too," Stevens said. "We're going to find out tonight who the oldest lady in the audience is. And we have a marvelous present for her."

The elderly women in the audience giggled in anticipation, while those who had attended the program before smiled knowingly.

"When we find the oldest lady," Stevens said with a convincing display of sincerity, "we're going to give her . . . the oldest *man*."

A hair-thin black indicator needle on the control board jumped all the way to the right side of a small dial as a shout of laughter blasted into the studio microphones.

"Don't laugh," Stevens continued. "The first time we tried this . . . I distinctly remember . . . was one night about ten years ago. We had a very nice lady in our audience. She was eighty-seven years old, as I recall. We introduced her that evening to a man from Chicago who was ninety-six and shortly thereafter, believe it or not, they were married. It was a lovely story. And that wasn't the end of it either. I read in the paper recently where that woman has just given birth to a beautiful forty-seven-year-old baby boy!"

"What time do we go on?" Dan said.

"First he does a few minutes by himself," Hank explained.

66

"Then he does a commercial or two, then he'll either bring us right out or else he'll go into the studio audience and do some interviews."

"That's my favorite part of the show," the engineer said. "Man, we don't know *what's* gonna happen out there. I have to keep my hand on this pot, too, because they come up with some pretty wild lines when he jumps down there with the hand mike."

"Well," Stevens was saying, looking carefully at his wrist. "It's about time to go on the air and I really don't know what I'm looking at here because my watch is in hock."

Hank said, "This guy's pretty off beat."

"He does things like that all the time," the engineer said. "Like the other night I put a cigarette into my mouth and Al holds up this lighter and begins clicking it, trying to give me a light and then all of a sudden I notice that it's not a lighter at all, just a house key that he's flicking with his fingernail."

The large clock on the control-room wall buzzed briefly, its minute hand wiggled and snapped smartly into the straight-up notch of twelve and Stevens said, "Ladies and gentlemen; we have a late news report from the CBS newsroom. The Kaiser's troops have just marched into Belgium!"

After the crowd had stopped chuckling, he said with a solemn face, "What's so funny? If that isn't the latest news report *you* ever heard I'll put in with ya. And I wonder where *that* expression originated. I'll put *what* in *where?*"

"This all done without script?" Dan said.

"One hundred per cent," the engineer said. "He just says whatever comes into his head."

"When does he go on the air?" Hank said, looking at the wall clock with a puzzled frown.

"We're already on," the engineer said.

"That's pretty weird," Hank said. "No announcer tonight?"

"Yeah, McGraw's here, but Al usually opens the show cold."

A tall plump man with a jovial expression walked onstage carrying a handful of papers and seated himself silently at a table upon which rested a microphone.

"Tom McGraw just sauntered in," Stevens said. "Tom, I hope I don't have to speak to you again about *sauntering*. I'll thank you to have the decency to *walk* like the rest of us, or else stride manfully, stalk determinedly, or even slouch dejectedly, but no more sauntering."

McGraw guffawed heartily. "All right, Al," he said. "To tell you the truth I don't think I was sauntering. Inasmuch as I was about five minutes late getting down here from upstairs I actually intended to *sneak* in."

"Then I'll thank you to wear your sneakers," Stevens said, adding, "There must be *something* I can thank you for."

"I can't imagine what it would be."

"Then," said Stevens, "I'll thank you to keep a civil tongue in your head—which is a scene from the picture *Where Else?* But I don't mind, Tom. If you've *got* a civil tongue you can keep it in a cigar box for all of me."

Seating himself suddenly at a concert piano, the lank comic played an arpeggio and sang "All of me—why not take all of me?"

"Jeez," Dan said. "This guy is the original Mr. Free Association."

"Yeah," Hank said. "He'll make more money out of stream of consciousness than Joyce ever did."

"Well," Stevens continued, "we've got some pretty interesting items in the old mailbag tonight. And why are the mailbags that radio people refer to invariably described as *old*? Same question goes for the old clocks on the wall. Someday I want to turn on my radio and hear a guy say, 'Well, folks, I see by the *new* clock on the wall that it's time to go.' But anyway, as I was saying when I was so rudely interrupted by my subconscious, we have a lot of interesting items in the mailbag tonight."

"Get many letters this week?" McGraw said.

"No," Stevens said. "No letters. Just interesting items. For example, I find in the old mailbag tonight two paper clips, four skrumbles of lint, and a—"

"Four whats of lint?" McGraw said, giggling.

"Tom," Stevens said, "I've got to hand it to you. (And don't drop it.) But your noticing the world skrumble—that shows you're paying attention. To tell the truth it's just a word I made up on the spot (and when you're on the spot you've got to do *something*)."

Hank lit a cigarette. "Half this guy's remarks," he said, "are made up of parenthetical clauses. He's closer to Proust than to Milton Berle."

Dan made a mental note to find out who the hell Proust was and resumed listening.

"Anyway," Stevens was saying "what would *you* call pieces of lint? The question, of course, is rhetorical and was submitted by an oracle named Rhett who will receive as a prize a handsome Bakelite, twenty-one jewel garter belt personally autographed by Roy Rogers and Trigger. Or, if this is not satisfactory, an unreasonable facsimile. Does that answer your question, Tom McGraw?"

"Look," McGraw said, "why don't you let me go through the formality of starting the show and then I'll get out of your way."

"You're not in my way, Tom," Stevens said. "But as for introducing the program, you can write your own ticket (if you remember to use carbon paper)."

McGraw made a formal announcement that it was time once again to present from Columbia Square that square from Columbia, Alan Stevens. The engineer piped in a recording of Stevens' theme "Laughing Boy" and when McGraw said, "And now here he is, your friend and mine, Alan Stevens," the audience applauded for Stevens for the second time.

"Hello there, friends and neighbors," Stevens said, "and how seldom neighbors are, now that I think of it. Well, let's get right to the mail. A lady in Pasadena wants to know if I really have to wear glasses or, as she so cleverly puts it, "Do you really have to wear glasses?" Well, no, only when I want to see. To tell you the truth I'm very nearsighted. In fact, I'm the only man in town who has to wear contact lenses to see his glasses.

"Now let's see. We have a card here from a man in—uh—in—cahoots. No, I mean in San Diego. (By the way, what are cahoots and how do you get in them? From the top, maybe? Or perhaps there's a little sliding panel in the side of the cahoot. A sliding cahoot panel, or as they would say in the army: Panel, cahoot, sliding, M-one.) But where was I? (And if it was nice there why did I move out?) Oh, yes. The man from San Diego. (Say, that sounds like a movie title, doesn't it? Republic Pictures presents John Wayne in *The Man From San Diego!* Coming!!! To your neighborhood meat market soon. You'll *thrill* as the usher punches you right in the mouth, *gasp* as the lobby drinking fountain squirts water up your nose!"

Stevens was speaking more loudly now, abandoning his stock radio suavity, getting wild, banging out mock movie-theme chords at the piano. The crowd was beginning to whoop it up with him, shouting encouragement.

"Christ," Hank said, laughing, "this is like a revival in a nut house."

"Yes," Stevens was exclaiming, "you'll see two thousand wild automobiles stampeding across an Arizona drive-in! You'll see five thousand hot dogs eaten alive by panicky suburbanites! You'll see ten thousand ants crawling all over a dropped Eskimo Pie! Don't fail to miss this monumental tribute to the brave men who pilot our elevators at the Broadway department store. See *The Man From San Diego*, starring John Wayne, Mabel Wayne, Bernie Wayne, Frances Wayne, pouring wain, soaking wet, and sick in bed! You'll be glad you did. Remember, it's the best friend your car ever had!"

At this, Stevens hit a sustained trumpet blast of a chord signifying that his impressionistic tirade was concluded.

CLOSING NIGHT AT THE INTERNATIONAL

(The following is a transcript of a routine that Allen ad-libbed the night he did his last late-night program from the old International Theatre on Columbus Circle in New York. It was a cool summer's evening in 1954. About fifteen minutes before the pro-

70

gram ended Steve picked up his hand mike and wandered down into the studio audience to explain to his viewers that the theatre was being torn down and that, starting the following night, his program would come from the Hudson Theatre on West 44th Street. A camera was set up outside on the street because Allen thought it would be interesting to finish with an exterior shot. As to just how he was to fill the final quarter hour, however, no one had any precise idea. The following is what actually happened.)

STEVE: I don't know if you people in the studio audience know (or even care), but you are here tonight under historic circumstances. This is the last program that will ever come from this, the old *International* Theatre. As a matter of fact, when this theatre was new they had different nations altogether.

For those of you who want to know where we will be broadcasting from next week, we will be coming from the Hudson.

Not the Hudson Theatre . . . the Hudson *River*. The situation is that bad.

We can't seem to get under a roof of any kind.

But they *are* tearing this joint down and I wasn't kidding. Immediately after the show this curtain goes for about $4.00 a yard.

A lot of folks have been writing in all week saying, "Why are they tearing down your nice theatre?" The reason is they are going to build a Coliseum on this spot. PFFT!! They're building a *big hole* on this spot; that's what they're doing.

I haven't read where the money has been appropriated yet, but they're being very destructive before they know for sure what they're going to build. But this *is* our last show here. Tomorrow night we will be coming from the Hudson, the theatre you step down into.

I want to express my sincere thanks to the members of the technical staff of the theatre, as distinguished from the network. Our stage crew, all the fellows who work in the building, have done a great job for us for the past several weeks. Thanks, fellas! (*No response*) I guess they're back there watching another program.

You probably saw the show Milton Berle did a week or so ago.

They are tearing down the theatre he broadcasts from too, the Center Theatre. Things are getting so bad several shows might have to come from one theatre. I can just see John Cameron Swayze hopscotching the world with Howdy Doody. It's going to come to that if we aren't careful.

(*In audience, to a visitor*): Who do you work for?

MAN: I work for Clark & Gibby.

STEVE: They were one of the best acts ever to hit the Loew's circuit. Remember them? Clark & Gibby? Remember that wonderful thing they did when they walked right out of the studio? Say, that gives me an idea. Will you hold this please?

(*Steve runs outside to the street; camera outside picks him up.*)

For years I have been wanting to do this. They are tearing this joint down tomorrow and eventually they will build a Coliseum here, and when they do we will be back at this address with an audience of twenty-four thousand people!

We are outside here now at Columbus Circle. Welcome to another broadcast of "You Are There." From here I can see that Columbus is just about to land and now we take you to Edward R. Murrow at the Central Park Zoo.

Oh, boy, this is fun out here! The buses are stopped. Hello, there. (*To people on bus, who looked on, puzzled*) Nice to see you.

What is this? (*Knocks on front of store that is all boarded up.*) I guess this is a *termite* store. (*He knocks on boards.*) You have just witnessed a scene from Danny Kaye's picture *Knock on Wood, and Break Your Whole Arm.* (*Reads signs on window.*)

"Jewelry Clearance Sale."

"Clearance Sale."

"Going Out of Business After Thirty-Three Years."

Very panicky—Sale.

Say, we have some good buys over here. And good-bye over there! Full-cut shorts, two for one dollar. That's only 25 cents a leg.

I'd better check these before I read them out loud or we will be off the air. (*Reads more signs.*)

This whole joint goes down tomorrow so, man, if you don't buy it tonight, you're dead!

(*Steve goes to door of clothing store. Looks in. People inside stare back at him, unsmiling.*)

Whoops. Hi. (*To camera*) They think I am coming in to buy something. (*To proprietor*) Hi. You are probably wondering who I am. Would you just step right out here on the sidewalk?

WOMAN: I bet you can't tell me what's my line?

STEVE: I'll handle the jokes, madam.

WOMAN: My husband runs the store.

STEVE: Well, it's a small world. Imagine running into him here tonight! And what's *your* name, sir?

MAN: Nat Silver.

STEVE: Nat Silver. Well Hi-Ho, Silver! Stretch out those long white legs of yours and come out here where there's a little more light.

(*Steve sees three men standing silently in store, looking on.*)

Who are those guys? Creditors?

MAN: No. I have no creditors.

STEVE: That's right, this "Last Week Sale" has been going on for several years now.

MAN: No, just two months.

STEVE: Well, I guess that's about the average.

(*Three men move in closer.*)

STEVE: Can you see them, folks? The Ritz Brothers.

Who *are* those fellows?

MAN: They are friends of mine. Three friends.

STEVE: All right. Three friends who shall be nameless. I just don't like the way they keep their hands in their pockets.

(*They are now outside on sidewalk.*)

Well, Mr. Silver, "This Is Your Life." (*Points to taxis at curb.*) We have thousands of cab drivers here that you have neglected to tip over the last fourteen years and they're coming back to see you.

No, I really don't know why I am out here except it's much cooler and I can get home a lot faster that way and get my make-up off before the audience finds out the show's over.

73

I hope you folks sell a lot of your underwear. When will you be out of the building?

MAN: We will be out Monday morning.

STEVE: Well, you're hanging on longer than *we* are.

MAN: I enjoy your program and watch it all the time.

STEVE: Well, tonight the program is watching *you!*

So it just shows you, if you play your cards right. . . . Well, good night, Mr. and Mrs. Silver and good night to Manny, Moe and Jack back there.

You know (*looks at merchandise*), they have some wonderful buys here, actually. I got some socks here yesterday for 29 cents a pair and they're terrific. They really are. No more of those 32-cent socks for *me*.

(*Steve walks up to passing pedestrian, a small, dark man apparently intoxicated.*)

STEVE: Your name, please?

MAN: Get outta here!

STEVE: This Is Your Life, sir!

MAN: (*Takes a swing at microphone.*)

STEVE: I bet you have *all* been wanting to do that for years, eh? Strike me down in my tracks! Well, I see by the Chevrolet sign that it is five minutes to twelve.

I might get a free minute hand for saying that.

(*Another drunk ambles up to Steve.*)

STEVE: How are ya?

(*Steve notices he is intoxicated.*)

STEVE: Oh, boy. Well, *who* are ya?

MAN: I am J. E. Taylor.

STEVE: Well, I'm J. Edgar Hoover and you're under arrest!

(*Steve notices police call box on light pole.*)

I am going to make a call here and pick up the secret word.

MAN: You're not going to call the police on me, are you?

STEVE: Of course, I'm not calling the police on *you*. *You're* not plugged in.

Well, I see our time is about up anyway so I guess I won't make any calls at all.

74

Thanks, Mr. Taylor, thanks, ladies and gentlemen for joining us in this open-air discussion tonight, and Merry Christmas to you all.

STEVE, GROUCHO AND CARL REINER

(Let's get back again to a discussion of comedy, humor and their relationship to Steve Allen and other comedians.

This time, however, there are others to do the talking for us. Thanks to a rough transcript that appeared in the April 4, 1960, edition of *Variety*, we can reproduce parts of a discussion in which Allen was involved.

Steve has always enjoyed the company of other comedians and is often at his best in such a context. The *Variety* report read as follows.)

As hilarious as any comedy of errors, the meeting Thursday night of the Academy of Television Arts & Sciences would have done the Bard proud. In its telescoped version—highlighted by the majority view that TV is getting the short end of comedy—it went something like this:

Setting: International Ball Room, Beverly Hilton Hotel.

Time: Thursday, March 31, 1960.

Characters:

Steve Allen

Groucho Marx

Carl Reiner

Cecil Smith, L. A. *Times* columnist

Robert Young

George Fenneman, panel moderator

The ballroom is filled to capacity. The lights dim as the spotlight falls on the moderator, who says . . .

FENNEMAN: We're here to discuss "Does the television industry take comedy seriously?" I'm not sure I know what the question means.

GROUCHO: (*Interrupting*) Fenneman, why aren't you home watching our show?

FENNEMAN: What makes a good comedian?

REINER: A comedian just happens. Sometimes it's environment. Sometimes heredity, like if you have a funny mother.

GROUCHO: I happen to be an illegitimate son. (*Laughter*)

ALLEN: Of *what*?

SMITH: In developing new talent, isn't it true that there's no place today for a comedian to be bad?

ALLEN: Sure there is. *Here!*

SMITH: Really. A young comedian goes on the "Ed Sullivan Show" in front of fifty million people, and you never hear of him again.

ALLEN: I'm glad to hear that.

FENNEMAN: I'm glad I had my dinner.

GROUCHO: I wish you'd had mine.

ALLEN: When does the duck come down?

SMITH: There are four comedians at this table . . .

GROUCHO: (*Interrupting*) Name one.

FENNEMAN: Are there any new television comedians?

GROUCHO: There's no new comedy because the networks won't allow comedians any freedom of speech. You can't do jokes about anyone. It's impossible to be funny unless you satirize and kid somebody. And there's no room for that on TV. Except Bob Hope, and he's a war hero.

ALLEN: New comedians do come along—like Mort Sahl, Elaine May and Mike Nichols, Lenny Bruce. But their talents aren't for television as it exists.

GROUCHO: Television gets exactly what it and the audience deserve. Good shows don't get ratings. I think there is the same junk on TV that there was ten years ago. Including my own show.

ALLEN: If things are to pick up, it must start with the sponsor.

REINER: Sponsors are afraid of comedians. They'd rather have anyone but a comedian fronting for their product. It's better to have someone like Loretta Young selling your automobile.

GROUCHO: She can't even drive.

ALLEN: Bob, what do you think?

REINER: How'd he get to be moderator?

76

YOUNG: I don't say this in defense of sponsors, but on last week's "TV Guide Awards Show," Chrysler let its auto commercial be spoofed. Growth of this sort is possible. At least this is an encouraging sign.

GROUCHO: It's the exception. The only way it will happen generally is in pay TV.

FENNEMAN: Here's a question from the audience on just that subject. Do you favor pay TV?

ALLEN: Let's take a poll of the audience.

FENNEMAN: How many are in favor? (*Strong applause*) Against? (*Weak applause*)

ALLEN: That's about 80 per cent in favor.

SMITH: On another subject . . . Groucho, are you a comedian?

GROUCHO: I don't consider myself a comedian. I'm just a man who asks a lot of questions, doesn't know most of the answers, and gives away prodigious amounts of money.

ALLEN: And *makes* prodigious amounts of money.

GROUCHO: And I save it all.

FENNEMAN: I know!

SMITH: Do writers have anything to do with the longevity of a comedian?

ALLEN: No. They're tremendously important, but if one writer quits, you hire another. Comedy, isn't a "thing"; it's an attitude. And it doesn't run out.

FENNEMAN: What about rating systems?

GROUCHO: They're absurd.

ALLEN: They're probably statistically correct, but they must be interpreted. The highest rating does not necessarily mean the best show.

GROUCHO: They should be investigated.

FENNEMAN: Here's a question for Steve. What's with Jack Paar?

ALLEN: Well, Hugh Downs is with Jack Paar.

FENNEMAN: Someone asks about violence on TV. I've seen things on TV you couldn't see in theatres.

77

GROUCHO: Like what?

ALLEN: Like the eleven o'clock "News."

FENNEMAN: Here's a note from someone. "Quit while you're ahead." Somehow I have a feeling we haven't answered the question.

(*Meeting adjourns for coffee*)

REMARKS AT CEDARS-MT. SINAI HOSPITAL DEDICATION CEREMONY
(WEDNESDAY, MARCH 27, 1974)

Thank you very much, ladies and gentlemen. This microphone seems to be much too low for me, and there's apparently no way to raise it.

I never realized that height could be a problem.

Well, it has certainly been exciting to listen to all the previous speakers and to take part in so important an event.

I admit that I *was* a bit startled when, in his opening remarks, Mr. Weinberg said that there were going to be "quite a few speakers." I thought he said "quite a few *streakers*."

[A photographer on his knees suddenly shot a flash picture.]

It's always interesting when a photographer runs up and shoots a picture up your nostrils.

You may take all the pictures of that kind you want, sir, but I do want you to know that they will be of interest only to the eye-ear-nose-and-throat department of this hospital.

As you may have noticed, I've been sitting here on the platform —for quite a long time, come to think of it—and jotting down notes as they occurred to me. In fact, I've been sitting here for so long that I now have enough material for a two-hour speech.

But having just written these observations I must confess I'm very anxious to hear them myself.

Seriously, it *is* an honor to be a part of these proceedings this morning because, when this institution is completed, it will attend to the medical needs of not only our local citizens but also our fighting men. The gas station owners.

78

Steve Broidy just referred to the fact that this morning culminates a ten-year effort and that is indeed the case. Think of it, my friends, ten long years, the last two of them spent listening to Mr. Broidy talk.

But I shouldn't complain; I'm lucky to be here at all. As you may have noticed, I drove in late, because I'm driving our *camper* rather than one of our cars, and I got lost a few blocks away from the place. I leaned out the window and said to a fellow standing on the sidewalk, "Where is Cedars-Sinai Hospital?" He said, "I'm sorry I can't help you; I'm a Christian Scientist."

I am not kidding; I really did have to drive the camper here this morning. My son's car was out of order so he drove Jayne's car to school. And Jayne took *my* car. So all that was left for me was either the camper or the motorcycle.

But I couldn't ride the motorcycle because I've just had my hair done.

But I must say a camper is a million laughs during a gasoline shortage.

But there it sits, right there in the parking lot. And after these proceedings are concluded this morning, ladies and gentlemen, if you'd just like to step over that way I'll be glad to take Chest X rays of all of you.

But in any event I *am* here now and—like all of you—I've been here a good long time.

In fact, we've been here so long that the lady in the red hat has taken *root*.

[A lady with a large flowery picture hat was seated in the audience.]

But this morning means a bit more to me than it might to some of you because I can remember back twenty-five years ago when a friend of mine was ill and told me he was going to Cedars of Lebanon. I went to visit him one day and discovered that there was no hospital—just *cedars*. He was sitting in the shade of one of them and making himself as comfortable as possible.

Actually they no longer call this institution Cedars of Lebanon. It's now—as you know—called Cedars-Mt. Sinai.

There still *is* a Cedars of Lebanon here in Los Angeles, however. That is now the name of Danny Thomas's house.

Ordinarily, at functions of this sort, I am assigned the task of making a few introductions. But Mr. Broidy has already done that. In fact, this is the first public meeting I've ever attended where every single person in the *audience* was introduced.

Since that's the case I'd like to introduce a few bystanders over there beyond the ropes. I see several former bootleggers and disbarred attorneys there and I'm glad to recognize them.

But just look at the skeleton of this building behind us, my friends.

[Seven or eight hardhats were gathered on an upper floor, looking on at the proceedings.]

Look at them up there. It looks like a Nixon commercial in the 1972 campaign.

Speaking of that, ladies and gentlemen, as I look at this audience this morning I see a great many extremely wealthy people of the Beverly Hills area. And I ask you people to just *think* of all the money you gave to Nixon in 1972—secretly or otherwise. If you'd given it to Cedars-Mt. Sinai, this place would have been finished two years ago.

Mr. Weinberg, when he introduced Dr. Charles Aronburg, the mayor of Beverly Hills, commented that it seemed odd to him that a doctor should also serve as a mayor. Personally I think it's a marvelous idea; it might be just what we need to attend to all of our sick cities.

Come to think of it, it would be better if we had more doctors in politics and a few less of some of those shady lawyers that have been causing so much trouble lately.

But all of us are here today because we realize the importance of the service that this great Cedars-Sinai Medical Center will provide. Think of the special features that this institution will provide. I wonder how many of you realize it will include the Ronald Reagan Wing.

That will be a special facility for the treatment of *botulism*.

FUN WITH COMMERCIALS

Although on the air Allen is usually the epitome of sincere sales-manship, his rehearsals are often brightened by the weird things he does to commercials, to amuse the members of his cast and crew.

Rather than try to explain the phenomenon let's just look at a commercial as written, and then as Allen did it in rehearsal.

AS WRITTEN:

Say, do you smear your youngsters like this when they have a chest cold? Gets your fingers pretty gooey, doesn't it? Well, you don't have to any more. Finally somebody has taken the grease and messiness out, and left just the helpful ingredients. Here's what I mean: It's called *Coldene Stick Chest Rub.* Watch how you avoid the messiness and discomfort of ordinary greasy rubs. Your fingers never even touch it. Looks like a giant lipstick, doesn't it? And with this new-type rub—*Coldene Stick*—there's no grease to get on your children, your fingers, pajamas, or bed sheets. No grease to hold back the medication in the rub. You get feelable relief in seconds, without messiness. And you can inhale the medication instantly. The full power of *Coldene Stick* goes to work faster to break up that painful congestion in the chest, throat, nose and sinus

ALLEN'S VERSION:

Say, do you smear your youngsters like this when they have a cold? Do they smear you right back? Gets pretty gooey; doesn't it? Well, friends, stick by those gooey kids of yours. They're the best friend your car ever had.

But finally somebody has taken the grease and messiness out, and put grit and grime back in.

Here's what I mean, and I wish I knew. It's called *Coldene Stick Chest Rub,* and you just stick it in your old rubbery chest. Watch how to avoid the messiness and discomfort of eating fried chicken with your bare hands. Your fingers never even touch it. That's right, the whole operation is handled by your toes.

Looks like a giant lipstick, doesn't it? So you folks with giant lips are really set. Remember, there's no grease to get on your children, but watch out for your mother-in-law.

You get feelable relief in

passages. Also rub *Coldene Stick* not only on the chest, but the nose and throat. And whenever you rub on *Coldene Stick* you'll notice that its medicated ingredients penetrate quickly through skin and deep into tissues. That's because there's no grease in *Coldene Stick Rub*. So to relieve a chest cold without messiness, get the new type rub . . . *Coldene Stick Chest Rub*. One dollar at all drugstores.

seconds. If not, that's show business.

And you can inhale the medication instantly. In fact, you can sit there and inhale it all day long for all I care. I warned you not to go out without a muffler!

The full power of *Coldene Stick* goes to work, signs in, takes a coffee break, quits at five o'clock, goes home from work again, takes off its shoes and hits you right in the mouth.

And it really breaks up congestion in throat, nose, scalp and the balls of the feet.

Remember, rub *Coldene Stick* not only on the chest but on the nose, the throat, the sternum, the atchison, topeka, and the santa fe.

There's no grease in the *Coldene Stick Chest Rub*. And that's not *all* that's missing.

Smoke a pack of them today. You'll be glad you did. One dollar at any filling station in town!

It's quite a shock for the men from Madison Avenue when they are first assigned to the Allen show and hear Steve massacring the pitches over which vice-presidents galore have labored long and lovingly. But by air time, Allen has gotten the kidding out of his system and the commercials are usually handled in straight-forward fashion.

AN UNFORGETTABLE MOMENT ON "WHAT'S MY LINE" (JOHN DALY'S GOOF ON MYSTERY GUEST SPOT, OCTOBER 4, 1964)

DALY: Sign in, please.
(*Applause*) (*Laughter*)

All right, panel. Just to remind Buddy Hackett, one question at a time, in turn, and we'll begin with Dorothy Kilgallen.

KILGALLEN: Are you a performer in show business?

ALLEN: Yeah . . . (*Elongated whisper*)

DALY: And now, Mr. *Allen* . . . OOPS!

("Oh" . . . "oh" [*Laughter*] ALL "oh" . . . ALL "oh") Mr. Cerf—

CERF: I'll make believe I didn't hear that.

DALY: You can't. Let's stop kidding.

CERF: Are you a comedian?

ALLEN: I'm not as funny as John is right now.

(*Applause*) (*Laughter*)

All right, Buddy. Three guesses. Who is it? Your time is up, Bud.

ARLENE: Can we come out now?

DALY: Considering the fact that I've opened up every door in the barn, there's no point in your staying in.

ALLEN: That's the first time that's ever happened to you, isn't it, John?

DALY: I've thought, over the fifteen years . . . one of these days, I'm going to do the silliest thing I could possibly do, and forget for a moment, and say the name of our mystery guest, and I did it tonight.

ALLEN: I'll tell you what, John; I'm going to take this up with Goodson and Todman, and I think instead of replacing Garry Moore, I'll replace *you*.

DALY: I've got a better idea. You know—now that you're on CBS every Monday night with that program, "I've got a great secret"; I wonder if *I* can apply.

ALLEN: Yes. John's secret is that he's out of a job.

BUDDY: John, Steve is one of the cleverest men in our business. Just let him go out and come back as somebody else.

AD LIBBING IN LAKE TAHOE AND LAS VEGAS (1964)

(The following are transcribed jokes ad-libbed in response to spontaneous questions from night-club audiences in Lake Tahoe and Las Vegas:)

Question: Why aren't you running in the gubernatorial race?
Answer: 'Cause I don't want to be gubernor.

* * *

Question: Last night I threw my *knee* out of joint doing the Watusi. Any suggestions?
Answer: Yes. Don't try the Black Bottom.

* * *

Fan: I find it hard to believe I'm actually talking to you.
S.A.: I find it incredible myself.

* * *

Question: How can you be on "I've Got a Secret" in New York tonight and here in Lake Tahoe at the same time?
Answer: Very simple. I am here in Lake Tahoe this evening on tape.

* * *

Question: I've got a quarter that says you don't know how to play "The World Is Waiting for the Sunrise."
Answer: What do you know about that; a guy with a talking quarter!

* * *

Question: Do you still play the licorice stick?
Answer: No, I had to give it up—I got diabetes.

* * *

Question: Do you look at women from the waist up or from the waist down?
Answer: Yes.

* * *

Question: What do you think of young men with long hair?
Answer: I often think they're young *women* with long hair.

* * *

Question: I'm twelve years old. What's in the midnight show that I'm not supposed to see?
Answer: Your father, kid.

84

* * *

Question: How would you prevent Lake Tahoe from becoming polluted?
Answer: I'd take away its liquor license.

* * *

Question: (*From a Thomas Allen of Concord, California*) Are you and I related?
Answer: Yes, but not to each other.

* * *

Question: When you worked at the Sahara Hotel in Las Vegas, what game of chance did you enjoy the most?
Answer: Trying to get my laundry back.

* * *

Question: The roast beef here was delicious. How's the ham?
Answer: I'm fine, thank you.

* * *

Question: Parlez vous français?
Answer: Nein.

* * *

Question: What do you think of a grandmother out with a younger man?
Answer: It depends on what she's out for.

* * *

Question: What advice would you give to two people who will be married shortly?
Answer: The big trick is to stay married longly.

* * *

Question: What is your wife's disposition early in the morning?
Answer: Unconscious.

* * *

Question: How'd you like to be in Richard Burton's shoes?
Answer: I'd rather be in his pajamas.

* * *

Question: Where were you and what were you doing when you thought of that great song "Gravy Waltz?"
Answer: I was sitting at my piano writing a song, as I recall.

* * *

Question: Are you Irish or Scotch or what?
Answer: I am half Irish, sir, and the way I'm going, by the time the show is over tonight I'll be half Scotch.

* * *

Question: Would you please talk up real loud, Mr. Allen? I'm sitting so far back in the room you look like you're on a seven-inch set.
Answer: The real cause of your difficulty, sir, is that I am, in reality, only two feet tall.

* * *

Question: Mr. Allen, is your son old enough for my daughter? She is eighteen.
Answer: These days *any*body's old enough for your daughter.

* * *

Question: When the heck will this show be over?
Answer: For you, right now!

* * *

Question: When is your wife going back with Jackie Gleason?
Answer: As soon as I go back with Portland Hoffa.

* * *

Question: Would you please say Happy Birthday to us? We are complete strangers who sat down at the same table this evening.
Answer: Well, isn't that nice. That reminds me of a couple who, when they came in here last night, had been married for twenty-three years and who, by the time they stood up to leave, were complete strangers.

86

* * *

Question: Mr. Allen, did you know that the Buick dealers are happy to be here tonight?
Answer: No, I didn't; but I know that the blackjack dealers are happy to *have* you here.

* * *

Question: How can I win at blackjack?
Answer: Use a real blackjack.

* * *

Question: What are your views on the mini-skirt?
Answer: I've been trying to get a better view of it for some time.

* * *

Question: What else do you play besides the piano?
Answer: The horses.

* * *

Question: What is the best way to break into acting?
Answer: Train yourself. I suggest three courses of study.
1. Acting lessons.
2. Tap dancing.
3. Political science.

* * *

Question: (*From a Rose Mary Nelson of Vallejo, California*) I am a redhead. Should I marry a blonde or a brunette?
Answer: Neither. You should marry a fella.

* * *

Question: Do you think I will win the five-hundred-dollar jackpot tomorrow?
Answer: No, but I think you'd better stop drinking tonight.

* * *

Question: Do rainbow trout in the Truckee River prefer flies or angle worms?
Answer: Neither. They prefer other rainbow trout.

* * *

Jayne: "Fight fire with fire," my mother used to say.
S.A.: Her mother was a fire-fighter.

* * *

Fan: Steve Allen, you're number one in my book.
S.A.: Let me know when your book's coming out.

* * *

Question: Weren't you the pre-curser of Jack Paar and Johnny Carson?
Answer: Yes. I cursed before any of them did.

* * *

Question: (*From a Mrs. Evertsen of Seattle.*) When are you coming up to God's country.
Answer: When I drop dead.

Chapter Three

TELEVISION SKETCHES

Look, up in the air! It can ad-lib and wisecrack in the manner of Groucho, pull crazy stunts like Harpo, play the piano and say crazy things like Chico. It's not a bird, it's not a plane, and not Superman, though it looks like Clark Kent. It's Steve Allen, supercomic. No wonder people say he is so many different persons—at times he seems to be all the Marx brothers rolled into one.

Allen has a natural sense for creating nonsense by uttering nonsensical words. On a Merv Griffin Show, ridiculing a hideous Los Angeles building, he said he wondered why when it was about to be erected someone didn't say "p'tooey." South American Fernando Lamas, also on the show, didn't understand what "p'tooey" meant. With his immediate sense of the absurd Steve explained "p'tooey" comes from the pituitary gland.

There's an adage in the field of law that a lawyer who defends himself has a fool for a client. One might say a TV comedian who wrote for himself would have a fool for a client. But if he were as magnificent a fool as Steve Allen creates that would be a masterful accomplishment. With television a vast wasteland, the zany spirit of Steverino, the wit and wisdom he possesses, are what is needed to restore comic fertility.

Like all the great TV comedians, Steve does, of course, use writers, but it is our good fortune that he often uses himself as writer. The following imaginative sketches have all been written by Allen himself.

"YOU BET YOUR BIRD"

(The following sketch, which Allen performed on the Ed Sullivan Show in the fall of 1964, is undoubtedly one of the wildest ever done on Sullivan's program. In fact it is probable that to this day not a few of Sullivan's regular viewers are unable to interpret what they saw the night Allen made a guest appearance with his one-time TV rival.

The sketch was unusual for Sullivan's format, for a number of reasons. First of all, it involves the humor of exaggeration refined to a point beyond the ridiculous. Secondly, it employed a large cast of cowboys, jugglers, dancing girls and boys, panel members, sound men and special effects artists.)

STEVE: I don't get much of a chance to watch daytime TV but whenever I do I notice that game shows are still popular.

But there's a difference between the quiz and panel shows of today and those of years ago. Remember the "64 Dollar Question" and "Information, Please" and "What's the Name of That Song?" All you had to do on programs like that was answer simple questions. But nowadays things are somewhat more complicated. Any day I expect to see something like this:

Music: Peppy quiz-show type theme.

Camera: Card with art work saying "You Bet Your Bird."

ANNOUNCER: Once again folks, it's time to play "You Bet Your Bird," and here's your Emcee, the ever-popular Johnny Ferndock.

Camera: We see a full-stage set. A panel with four chairs is on

*one side. A podium for the emcee is center stage. There is an
enormous screen upstage which is divided into many squares.
Some of these must light up. Running down the left side of this
screen is a list of names of birds. Canaries, sparrows, cockatoos,
parakeets, bluebirds, eagles and dodos.*

*Across the top of the screen run the names of cities: Pomona,
Las Vegas, Kansas City, Chicago, Waukegan, Birmingham and
Miami Beach.*

STEVE: Hi, folks. Once again it's time to play "You Bet Your
Bird," and there's a lot of excitement tonight because our Jack
Pot Nest Egg is up to fifty-seven thousand dollars! Now I see our
four contestants are ready, so let's run down the rules. Contestant
Number One, Mrs. Melnick, has decided to be a *parakeet*.

Music: Sting

Contestant Number Two, Mr. Pasternak, has decided to be a
cockatoo.

Music: Sting

Number Three, Mr. Lishness, is a *canary*.

Music: Sting

And Number Four, Mr. Tishman, is a *dodo*.

Music: Sting

Now the object of the game is to get your bird all the way to
Miami Beach, by answering a series of questions. The only thing
is, you can*not* give your answer in *English*.

If you know the answer to a question you put up your right
hand and wave your handkerchief, at the same time screaming
"Caw, caw!!"

Whoever raises his handkerchief *first* is entitled to a wonderful
prize: two glorious weeks in the lobby of the Pantages Theatre!

If your answer is correct, then you light up the Bird Board.
Like this!

Camera: Big screen begins flashing and lighting. Fireworks go off.
Sound: Bell rings and machine-gun fire is heard.

But, if your answer is *wrong* then we take away your handkerchief and you have to wave your underwear!

Now if any of the other contestants want to *challenge* your answer, they press the challenge button—and if you gave the wrong answer then we turn to the big Bird Board and watch in horror as your bird is destroyed in midflight. Like this!

Camera: We see one of the birds on the big screen move forward about a foot. Suddenly it blows up. Feathers fly through the square where the bird was. They drift down. A dark brown liquid begins to drip down the front of the big board.

STEVE: When your bird is blown up this means that a certain amount of bird gravy will begin to drip down the front of the big Bird Board. If within ten seconds it drops down to the second level that means you get another chance. You must immediately switch to another bird and prepare to take off for points East.

The *ladies* on the panel must remember that they are to give their answers in Rumanian, after we put the famous "paper bag" over their heads. If, after thirty seconds under the bag, they can still breathe they are to indicate this by screaming, "I am a drake and you are a duck. Quoth the raven: Lotsaluck."

When the men on the panel hear the word *raven,* they are to stand up, kiss the nearest screaming woman on her paper bag, all the while saying, "Ladybird, ladybird, fly away home. Your house is on fire, you may borrow my *comb.*"

Then, when the lady *takes* the gentleman's comb she guesses the number of teeth in it. If she is *correct* she *keeps* the comb! If she is *wrong* she goes right over to our famous *Dentist's Chair* and sits down and opens her mouth. While she is in the chair she has her choice of either novocaine or laughing gas. If she chooses laughing gas she gets ten points. This sends her bird all the way to Las Vegas. If she chooses novocaine she gets twenty points, but this sends her bird only as far as Pomona.

In the meantime we play our mystery melody. Les, let's *hear* a little of the mystery melody.

Effect: Play a tape backward. Four seconds.

STEVE: That's it. Any contestant who knows the name of the

92

mystery melody leaves his seat and runs over here to the Fallout Shelter. If the other contestants try to get into the shelter after him he picks up a shotgun and lets them have it.

Our original contestants are laid to rest in the bird sanctuary and if that happens then our Jack Pot Nest Egg jumps to 150 thousand dollars and we get four *new* contestants who have been kept warm in the incubator section of our studio audience. These people are selected on the basis of being lassoed at random by Ragtime Cowboy Joe.

Camera: A cowboy runs out, throws a rope into audience. Cut to shot of four people roped. They are dragged to stage and stand over to one side.

STEVE: These contestants are given a chance to identify the Mystery Bird Dance. All right, Mystery Bird Dancers, lets have it.

Music: Weird music.

Four dancers come in. Do fast and eccentric dance, then freeze.

STEVE: If one of our contestants knows the name of the dance he sticks out his tongue and yells.

At this point we take Contestant Number Two and ask *him* the big Bird Board question. (*The two men involved now are actually jugglers. They are given flaming torches which they proceed to throw back and forth to each other.*) If he knows the answer he is called into active military service, but if he does not then he must face the Executioner!

Music: Mysterioso phrase.

(*A hooded man in black executioner's garb appears. He too is a juggler.*)

The Executioner stands by while the contestant tries to answer the remaining questions. If he fails, then the Executioner throws the flaming torches at him. If he cries out in pain, he forfeits not only the prize money but 45 per cent of his income for the next four years.

(*The torches begin to fly back and forth.*)

At this point we resume not only the Mystery Bird Dance but the Mystery *Melody* and those contestants still conscious who can estimate our rating within three points must join in the dance itself until death do us part.

And now we're ready to play "You Bet Your Bird."

ANNOUNCER: I'm sorry, Johnny, but we've run out of time.

STEVE: Really? Oh, that's too bad. But folks, be sure to tune in *next* week at which time we will resume our explanation of the rules for playing "You Bet Your Bird." And later in the season we hope to get around to actually playing the game.

Night all!

Music: Bird dance with full company

THE WEDDING OF BIG STEVE AND MISS JAYNIE

MERV GRIFFIN: You know, years ago the custom in radio and TV was that one network would not even acknowledge the *existence* of another. But today that's all changed. Take these late night shows. I don't mind referring to Johnny Carson or Joey Bishop or Dick Cavett or whoever . . . and Johnny and the rest of them will refer to *our* show.

So, we all know that a few nights ago Tiny Tim and Miss Vickie were actually married on Johnny's show. But—not to be outdone—I'm very proud to tell you that tonight there's going to be a wedding on *our* show.

STUDIO GANG: (*Whoops it up. Applause. Whistles. Huzzah, etc.*)

MERV: Yes, that's right. Tonight's the night you've all been waiting for . . . the night when that famous falsetto singing star *Big Steve* gets married to lovely fourteen-year-old *Miss Jaynie!*

STUDIO GANG: (*More Hoorays. Wowie, etc!*)

MERV: But wait now. Calm down. Remember, this is a very *dignified* occasion and we must conduct this service in the *best of taste*. So watch yourselves at all times.

And now . . . the *wedding of Big Steve and Miss Jaynie.*

Music: Organ, Methodist Style. "In Days Gone By"

Camera: Cut to wide shot of double doors and wall paneling. Set should include flowers, wispy curtains, etc. After four or five seconds the doors swing slowly open. What we now see is another set of double doors. After a few seconds they swing slowly open. We now see a third set of doors. They open too. Jayne and Bride's father are standing with backs to us. After a moment they realize they are on, do a take or two, and Jayne indicates to dumb father that they are headed the wrong way. They stop walking away from us, turn around and start slowly toward us.

(Production note: On our show I would get two funny-looking women from our audience and have them serve as flower girls, but it's not necessary.)

As bride and father near downstage mark, the minister, and Big Steve come in together, arm in arm. The minister suddenly realizes Steve is holding his arm and slaps his hand away. Steve has long dark hair and a prominent nose.

They all take their places. The minister is naturally wearing clerical attire, a fancy robe.

Music: Organ is continuing to play under all the above. Now it diminishes in volume and after a few seconds stops.

MINISTER: *(Jack Carter) (He speaks with great solemnity.)* Dearly Beloved . . . we are gathered here . . . in Studio 43 . . . in the *(Looks up)* sight of cameramen, stagehands and sensation seekers—to join these two—these two—*people (He is not quite sure what they are)* in a long-term contract, with two years firm . . . with options.

Who giveth thith . . . *this* bride away?

FATHER: I giveth. And it'th about time.

JAYNE: *(Smiles sweetly at Father in a close-up.)*

FATHER: Thith—*this* lovely child being but fourteen years per annum, parental conthent . . . *consent* is duly given.

MINISTER: Yours of the twenty-second received and contents duly noted. Dearly beloved . . . we are gathered here . . . to increase our rating . . . in this highly competitive situation. And if any man shall know reason why these two—these two—*people (His eyes roll to the ceiling)* should *not* be joined together let him speak now, mindful that he is watched over by the holy Spiro Agnew.

FATHER: (*He steps forward and tries to hand the minister the ring.*)

MINISTER: (*Under his breath*) Not *yet*, you idiot!

FATHER: Oh, I'm sorry. Well, I'm anxious to get this thing over with; I'm double-parked.

JAYNE: Father, *please*. (*She gives him an elbow in the ribs.*)

FATHER: (*He doubles up in pain. Grimaces silently*)

MINISTER: Now then. Does the groom have anything to state, for the record?

STEVE: Yes. I would like to announce that I have completely rewritten the marriage ceremony myself, with knowledge aforethought and considerable chutzpah.

MINISTER: Amen. Having revised a ceremony that has stood inviolate . . . and in several other shades as well . . . for five centuries, would you explain to our far-flung viewing audience, in what *particulars* you have made changes?

STEVE: Yes. Instead of me repeating after *you* . . . *you* will repeat after *me*.

MINISTER: Listen, you're paying for this.

FATHER: No, *I'm* paying for this.

MINISTER: By the authority invested in me by the vest I'm wearing, can we get this show on the road?

STEVE: Very well. Repeat after me.

MINISTER: Repeat after me.

STEVE: No, not *yet*.

MINISTER: No, not *yet*.

STEVE: Will you *stop!*

MINISTER: Oh, I'm sorry.

STEVE: All right. Oh, I could scream. Now then. Being of sound mind.

MINISTER: (*At that he breaks up.*)

FATHER: It struck *me* funny, too.

JAYNE: Father, *please!*

(*She gives him another painful elbow in the stomach.*)

96

FATHER: (*He doubles up silently.*)

STEVE: Being of sound mind.

MINISTER: Being of sound mind.

STEVE: Sound of limb and strong of wind.

MINISTER: Sound of limb and strong of wind.

STEVE: I promise not to be puffed up.

MINISTER: Not to be puffed up.

STEVE: Not all swollen and baggy-eyed.

MINISTER: Not all swollen and baggy-eyed.

STEVE: Slow to anger.

MINISTER: Slow to anger.

STEVE: Quick to snicker.

MINISTER: Quick to snicker.

STEVE: First in war.

MINISTER: First in peace.

STEVE: And first in the hearts of his countrymen. One if by land.

MINISTER: Two if by sea.

FATHER: And I on the opposite shore shall be.

STEVE: Being of sound mind.

MINISTER: I wish you wouldn't keep stressing that.

STEVE: Roses are red.

MINISTER: Violets are blue.

STEVE: Jim Aubrey's back.

MINISTER: And how are you?

Now that I have the idea, will the bride repeat after *me*.

JAYNE: Repeat after *me*.

FATHER: Not *yet*, stupid.

MINISTER: Being a big record fan.

JAYNE: Being a big record fan.

MINISTER: I promise to cleave, cling, clutch and grab.

JAYNE: I promise to cleave, cling, clutch and grab.

MINISTER: For richer or poorer.

JAYNE: For richer or poorer.

MINISTER: On Decca or Victor.

JAYNE: On Decca or Victor.

MINISTER: On Donder and Blitzen.

JAYNE: On Donder and Blitzen.

MINISTER: In sickness and in wealth.

JAYNE: In sickness and in wealth.

MINISTER: By hook or by crook.

JAYNE: By hook or by crook. With community property.

MINISTER: With community property.

JAYNE: Forsaking my Beatles albums and weird posters.

MINISTER: Forsaking my Beatles albums and weird posters.

JAYNE: Leaving behind forever my Clear-a-cill.

MINISTER: Whatever you say.

JAYNE: I swear by Tom Jones.

MINISTER: Make it easy on yourself.

JAYNE: To love, honor and do my homework.

MINISTER: To love, honor and do my homework.

JAYNE: For as long as I can.

MINISTER: You said a mouthful. The ring apparently having been stolen, I now declare you Nichols and May.

You may now kiss the bride.

FATHER: (*He starts to kiss Jayne.*)

MINISTER: Not you, stupid.

STEVE: (*He tries to kiss Jayne but, as the camera reveals in a rather close shot, his nose keeps getting in the way and they can't quite get their mouths together.*)

STEVE: Well, never mind, Miss Jaynie. We can have your mouth fixed.

Cue: Applause

Organ: Wedding March. The concluding one.

(*The bride and groom go over and sit in the two chairs to the right of Merv.*)

MERV: Well, Big Steve, *congratulations!* I must say that the ceremony was conducted with great dignity. It was very lovely.

STEVE: Thank you, Mervie. I'll always be grateful to you for this. After all, you gave me my start. And I think the American people are going to remember that for a long time.

MERV: Oh, it was nothing.

STEVE: That may be.

MERV: Where will you be going on your honeymoon, Miss Jaynie?

JAYNE: Well, *first* I have to find out if Daddy will let me cross the street. But I *would* like to thank all the people who made this possible (*Reads from a list on a card.*) *Loretta Harris*, who did my *hair*. Unfortunately I wasn't there at the time.

STEVE: Yes, honey, and I'd like to thank Miss Loretta for doing *my* hair, too. And I'd like to thank *Mr. Tough-guy*, for designing my wardrobe. And *Raymond Loewey Associates*, for designing my nose.

MERV: Will you and Miss Jaynie be doing any *work* together?

STEVE: Yes, Mervie. I'm going to star her in a new *picture* I'm producing.

MERV: What's it called?

STEVE: *Jail Bait.*

MERV: Sounds interesting. By the way, Big Steve, how many children do you plan to have?

STEVE: Just one. Miss Jaynie here. She'll be my only child.

JAYNE: Oh, Big Steve, darling, why don't you sing the little song you wrote for me!

STEVE: All right, Miss Jaynie.

JAYNE: By the way, sweetheart, you can stop calling me "Miss" now.

STEVE: I can? *Why?*

JAYNE: We're *married*.

STEVE: We *are?*

JAYNE: Yes.

STEVE: (*He faints and slips from his chair*)

Music: The drummer does schtick to emphasize his slump.

JAYNE: Big Steve, wake up, darling!

STEVE: Oh. I'm all right. I just did that to be funny.

JAYNE: Well, it wasn't.

STEVE: Now, now, Miss Jaynie. Remember, you don't have the greatest sense of humor in the world.

JAYNE: Listen, buster, I not only have a great sense of humor, I have a signed document that *proves* I have a sense of humor.

STEVE: What's that?

99

JAYNE: Our marriage license.
You'd better sing the song, sweetheart.

STEVE: Okay. (*He plays a little ukulele, perhaps the windup type.*)
"She stood on the bridge at midnight
 Disturbing my sweet repose,
 For she was a young mosquito
 And the bridge was the bridge of my nose."

MERV: You wrote that for Miss Jaynie? Do you have one more?

STEVE: Yes, Mervie. Here's one I wrote for her on our wedding day.

JAYNE: Sweetheart. That's *today*. We just got married.

STEVE: We did?

JAYNE: Yes.

STEVE: (*He faints again.*)

Music: Drum Schtick

(*As he wakes up*) Gosh, to think that we've been married now for four minutes and thirty-seven seconds.

JAYNE: And they said it wouldn't last.
Sing, darling. You've got a great set of pipes.

STEVE: You like my voice, angel?

JAYNE: No. But your *pipes* are okay.

STEVE: Just for that, here's a song I wrote about my first girl friend. Her name was Ruth.
"Ruth rode on my motorcycle
 On a seat in back of me.
 I took a bump at 95
 And rode on Ruthlessly!"

(*Steve and Jayne rise on applause, [Exit music.] Throwing kisses in all directions as they disappear.*)

THE PRICKLY HEAT TELETHON

Scene: Typical telethon setup. Double-level panel with pretty girls and second-rate actors answering phones. Small band area on Stage Left. Master of Ceremonies works in center.

Large backdrop sign says:
National Association for Prickly Heat
14th Annual Telethon
On Stage Left is large board with numbers that will give money
totals through the evening.
Music: "We're Having a Heat Wave." Very corny, show-opening
style. Up and fade for announcer's voice.

ANNOUNCER: From the heart of Manhattan into *your* hearts, ladies and gentlemen, it's the fourteenth annual Prickly Heat Telethon, bringing you the greatest names in show business, in a special fund-raising program that kicks off this year's campaign against prickly heat. And here is your master of ceremonies, Dennis Allen.

STEVE: (*Enters*) Thank you, Bob, and hello, America. Well, sir, here we are with the big annual Prickly Heat Telethon, and once again we're depending on you good people out there to stay up all night . . . miss work in the morning . . . call us on the telephone . . . make your pledges . . . send in that money, tote that barge, lift that bale, and help stamp out this terrible scourge, prickly heat.

We've got a lot of the biggest names in the business over here on the phones, waiting for your calls. I mean people like Conrad Nagel, Helen Twelvetrees, Guinn "Big Boy" Williams and Barton MacLane!

Camera: Loose pan of double-layered panel as Steve mentions
names. Not too tight.

STEVE: Farciot Eduardot, Lionel Atwill, Slim Summerville, and Honeychile Wilder!

Imagine that, these wonderful people, some of whom came out of retirement this evening, to spend a few hours here with you, mooching drinks and sandwiches all night long, great troupers that they are.

Yes, we cleaned out the Lambs Club, ladies and gentlemen, to bring you this star-studded lineup! Now remember, our goal this year is two million dollars! At the moment let's see how much we've raised in pledges and contributions! The first total is—

Music: Trumpet fanfare.
Camera: Show money board as numbers spin. A weird-looking girl in tights—Ruth Buzzi—smiles inanely.
STEVE: Seventy-six cents! Seventy-six, that's the spirit, folks! Remember, prickly heat can strike anywhere. On the nape of your neck. Behind the knees. In the small of your back. It can strike without regard to race, creed or nationality. So give until it hurts. Remember, the itch you save . . . could be your own.

Do you realize, my friends, that a man gets prickly heat in the city of New York every twenty-nine seconds. We have that man here tonight!
Camera: Pan to man who sits scratching like hell.
STEVE: He's dead game, ladies and gentleman, and I know you're greatly impressed with his courage. So keep those phone calls coming in. In New Jersey, the number to call is Epidermis 4-9678. (*Super number in white.*) And on Long Island the number is Soothingsalve 5-7000. (*Super number.*)

And now, let's get to a little entertainment here, folks. I give you a very clever young comic, who has just come over here between shows from the Copacabana, in downtown Boise, Idaho. That very witty, snappy young funster, let's welcome the King of Mirth . . . Lenny *Jackie!*
Music: "Fine and Dandy." Up and fade.
COMIC: (*John Byner*) Thank you, Dennis, and good evening, ladies and germs. I wanna tell you, it's great to be here for this great cause, whatever it is.

What is this, an audience or an oil painting? Ha-ha-ha! Yes, sir! I just want to tell ya . . . a funny thing happened to me on the way to the studio tonight. A bum came up to me and said, "Say, buddy, I haven't had a bite in three days!"

Then there was the time when these two Armenians got off a streetcar in downtown Boston. I know you're out there, folks, I can hear you breathing.

And now I'd like to give you my impression of Lionel Barrymore. (*He turns away and then back.*)

Listen, Jocko—you're the guy—who gave it to my brothah—in the back.

Don't applaud, folks. Just throw money.

But seriously, folks . . . I don't have to do this for a living. I can always sell tennis shoes to Howard Hughes. These are the jokes. (*To Steve*) Too smart for the room, Dennis. Going right over their heads.

Come on, folks, laugh it up; I laughed at *you*.

People are crazy today. Take my wife . . . please. And that's why I say:

Music: Slow two-beat Dixie tag phrase

Just keep laughing . . . keep smiling . . . Right in your mouth!

Music: "Fine and Dandy" again. Very fast.

COMIC: (*He runs back for four million bows. Steve cannot get him off.*)

STEVE: How about that, folks? Isn't that a great talent? Oh, by the way, we'd like to thank Sam of Sam's Delicatessen, for all the sandwiches and coffee which are being served here tonight. Sam, come over here and take a bow.

SAM: (*Louie Nye*) Thank you, folks. Thank you, Dennis. I just want to say that I'm behind this thing 100 per cent. I know what a terrible scrooge prickly heat is . . . and—

STEVE: Not scrooge. Scourge!

SAM: It's that, too!

Because I feel this thing so strongly . . . in my heart . . . I am personally *giving* you all these sandwiches and coffee and leftovers this evening. At cost!

STEVE: How about that, Sam! Beautiful. Thank you so much. Okay. What's the new total now? The total *is*!

Music: Fanfare:

A dollar and a quarter!!

Well, we're getting off to a sort of slow start with our telethon this evening, but I know you're not going to let us down, are you, folks? Remember, one person in twenty will get prickly heat this year. And he'll give it to the other nineteen, if I know these people.

So there's no getting away from this thing. It's reached epidemic proportions. If you don't believe me, perhaps you'll take the word of our medical adviser, the eminent physician Dr. Seymore Clyde.

DOCTOR: (*Dayton Allen*) (*He enters, dressed like a nut and walks right off the other side of the stage. Eventually he is located.*) Good evening, Dennis.

STEVE: Dr. Clyde, you are the head of the National Prickly Heat Drive, aren't you?

DOCTOR: Yes, Mr. Allen, and I just want to tell your audience that the fight against prickly heat can be won. The secret is in research. Some doctors don't understand this. I know one surgeon who treated a patient for two years for kidney trouble . . . and two years later that patient died of *heart* trouble.

STEVE: Really?

DOCTOR: Yes! But not with me. If I treat you for kidney trouble you *die* of kidney trouble!

STEVE: I see.

DOCTOR: And you don't have to wait two years to do it, either.

STEVE: At the present time, doctor, you are the *head* of the National Prickly Heat Institute, are you not?

DOCTOR: Who says I'm not! Of course I am. I *discovered* prickly heat, many years ago. I got a *patent* on it. Anybody wants this thing, they got to come to me. I got a corner on it.

STEVE: How did you get started in the field?

DOCTOR: Well, I didn't start in the field, Dennis. I started in a hospital.

STEVE: But when you started working on prickly heat . . .

DOCTOR: I started from scratch, believe me.

STEVE: But can we now beat this thing?

DOCTOR: No. I wouldn't recommend that. Maybe you could rub it a little. But no beating.

At the first sign of an attack, take two aspirins and get in bed. If pain persists or is unusually severe, well, that's the breaks of the game.

But just to show you my heart's in the right place I am going to make a donation to this cause myself tonight.

STEVE: How's that?

DOCTOR: I am not going to charge you for this call.

STEVE: Thank you, doctor, and good night.

Well, now, let's go over to the telephone panel here. They say a lot of calls are coming in. (*He crosses to people at panel.*)

Right here we've got that great picture star, Mr. Chuck Roast. Evening, Chuck,

CHUCK: Evening, Dennis. (*He is on the phone.*) I'm handling a call here. What is your name, sir? (*He makes notes.*) Lyle Socks? And you're giving ten dollars? Wonderful. Where are you calling from, Lyle? Oh, the other end of the panel?

Camera: (Pull back to show other actor down the line)

LYLE: Yes, I'm down here, Chuck. How are you?

CHUCK: Fine, Lyle. How's yourself?

STEVE: Well, let's move along here. Right here we have that lovely lady of the silver screen, Lila Lipstick.

ACTRESS: (*Jayne Meadows*) Hello, Mr. Allen, darling. It's so wonderful to be here for this *adorable* disease.

STEVE: Well, it's great to have you, Miss Lipstick.

ACTRESS: Thank you. I'm glad to take part in this campaign because, you see, this is my favorite disease.

And I know what I'm talking about, too, because we had prickly heat in my own family.

STEVE: Oh? On your father's side or your mother's side?

ACTRESS: No, on *my* side. (*She scratches her side to show him.*) Could I mention my latest picture?

STEVE: Certainly. What is it?

ACTRESS: I forget.

STEVE: Good. And now, folks, look who's taking phone calls. That wonderful black actor, George Token. Hi, George, listen, next time do me a favor. Don't sit in the back of the panel.

(*A child approaches.*) Well, what have we here?

SMALL BOY: Mr. Allen, I've been watching your show and I wanted to do something to help the fund-raising drive.

STEVE: That's wonderful, sonny. Bless your heart! You're a little scout of some kind. Have you raised some money?

BOY: Yes, I have, sir. I went all over the neighborhood and asked people for money. And I broke open my piggy bank.

STEVE: Isn't that wonderful, folks? Imagine that!

BOY: You see, my mother and father had prickly heat.

STEVE: Ah, you poor kid.

BOY: Yes, and they were so busy scratching, they didn't have much time for me.

So anyway I raised this money and here it is.

(*He hands him a few coins.*)

STEVE: How much is it?

BOY: Twenty-seven cents.

STEVE: (*He shoves the kid.*) Get off the stage, you little crum!

Get this punk outta here!

Stop that kid. He's stealing a cookie back there!

And now I'd like to introduce once again, that lovely lady of the silver screen, Lila Lipstick.

JAYNE: (*Enters*) Good evening again, Dennis. It's wonderful to be here with you tonight for this worthy cause.

I'd like to sing for all you wonderful people a song from my latest album:

FORGETTING

"I can't forget that you've forgotten me.
Please don't forget that I forgot to forget you.
You forgot that I forgot
To forget the night we met.
I forgot you were so pettable;
It was all so unforgettable.

We can't forget what we forgot before
And when forgetting is forgotten once more,
If your heart forgets, well, let it
If you've forgotten me, forget it,
I forgot that you're forgetting me yet
I forgot what I'd forgotten to forget."

STEVE: (*Walks in, gives her a disgusted look.*) Forget it.

JAYNE: But I'm not finished.

STEVE: That's what you think.

And now, folks, let's get back over here to the panel and meet some of these other wonderful celebrities.

Why, look who's there! It's one of your favorite Hollywood leading men, ladies and gentlemen, Mr. Gear Shift. Good evening, Gear.

GEAR: Good evening, Dennis. It's wonderful to be here with you tonight.

STEVE: Let's see, Gear. You want to tell the folks what your latest picture is?

GEAR: Well, actually, Dennis, I haven't made a picture in quite some time. But I'm working quite steadily.

DENNIS: Oh, really? On Broadway?

GEAR: No.

STEVE: In a TV series?

GEAR: No. I work mostly on these telethons. Tonight I'm here with you to help stamp out prickly heat, and then I just came back from Portland, Oregon, where I appeared on their annual Flat Feet Telethon. That goes over very big up there, you know. There are a lot of people who suffer from flat feet and they're trying to stamp out flat feet.

That joke got nothing in Portland, by the way.

But all seriousness aside . . . two weeks ago I MC'd another wonderful telethon in Cedar Rapids, Iowa. It was the big annual *Halitosis* Telethon. We're trying to wipe out bad breath, you know. It can strike anywhere, and I wish you'd move back a little bit, Dennis, now that I think of it.

We got a few complaints from the garlic people, but in general, the people back in Cedar Rapids were really behind us.

And I'm glad a lot of them weren't in *front* of us, I'll tell you that.

STEVE: Where will you be working next, Gear?

GEAR: Well, next week, Dennis, I fly to Boise, Idaho, for their big annual *Hoof-and-Mouth Disease* Telethon. It is the second greatest killer of cattle, you know.

STEVE: Oh? What is the *first* killer?

GEAR: We are, Steve. *People.* Yes, it's terrible, but people kill more cattle by far than hoof-and-mouth disease ever could. I'm thinking of organizing an Anti-People Telethon next year. I think eventually we've got to stamp out people, even at the risk of putting myself out of work in the long run. But there *are* some things that are bigger than a man's career.

STEVE: Well, thanks very much, Gear Shift, and I know you're going to stay right here on the telephones all night. We'll be looking for you on local TV around the country during the next few weeks.

Now, let's see what our grand total is as we go to the tote board.

Camera: Show total board

STEVE: The total is . . .

Music: Fanfare

Twenty-seven dollars and fourteen cents!

May I remind you, ladies and gentlemen, that our objective is two million dollars! Now, please! Keep those calls and pledges coming in! (*He is beginning to get nasty.*) Wait a minute, I've just been given a note that tells me we have a large donation coming in, and here to make that donation in person is one of the leaders of the business community, Mr. Phil—or "Filthy," as his friends call him—Rich. "Filthy" Rich. Come on out here, Phil.

RICH: (*He enters, burning a dollar bill with the end of his cigar or cigarette lighter.*) Good evening, Dennis.

STEVE: Good evening, Mr. Rich.

RICH: You can call me "Filthy."

STEVE: Tell me, Filthy, how much is it you're prepared to donate this evening?

RICH: Well, Steve, I know what a serious problem prickly heat is. It's kind of gotten under my collar, you might say. Now I want nothing in return for this marvelous gesture I'm making. But I want you to know that my firm stands behind me as I present this check to you tonight.

By my firm, I mean of course, the Rich Manufacturing Company, located at 1769 Longbranch Avenue in Teaneck, New Jersey, where the New Jersey turnpike meets Highway 29, and we're open twenty-four hours a day to welcome you to our lovely showrooms.

STEVE: Well, thank you, Mr. Rich. Actually we're not permitted to broadcast commercial messages, and I was just wondering if—

RICH: Oh, I have no selfish motive in coming here tonight, Dennis, I assure you. My company—which has branches in thirty-eight states—certainly wants to make this donation for this wonderful cause. Remember, folks, we're open from eight in the morning till three o'clock the next morning, working around the clock for your dining and dancing pleasure.

Come in and place a down payment. Ask about our lay-away plan. Some of our salesmen speak Spanish. Special courtesies extended to prickly heaters. We are an equal-opportunity employer. Vets, no money down.

If you have suffered from prickly heat, we'll put you on our training program so that you can work on our assembly line with one hand while you're still doing a little scratching with the other.

STEVE: Thank you very much, Mr. Rich. I was wondering exactly how much your donation—

RICH: I personally am making my donation anonymously, Dennis. We've all got to get behind this thing and put it over big. Everybody at our main showrooms out in Teaneck is looking in tonight. Hi, Harry. Hi, Mable. I'm on TV.

STEVE: Mr. Rich, we're running a little short of time. May I see your check? What is the size of it?

RICH: Here is the check, Dennis. And now I'll say good night, folks. We look to see all you people soon at our main showrooms in Teaneck. Drop in and tell them that Phil Rich himself sent you.
(*He exits.*)
(*Steve looks at check.*)

STEVE: Twelve dollars and fifty cents.
(*He crumbles check and throws it on floor.*)

And now on with our show. Let's check the clock and see what *time* it is.
(*He looks at clock on the wall.*)

Well, it's four in the morning. We've been on for two days, and we're still going strong. And now again, it's time for entertainment. A lot of wonderful people are donating their services to keep you folks entertained, and our next guest is seen regularly with his own early morning show on Station W-Oy-Vey. Here is Goofo, the Clown. Come out here, Goofo.

(*Goofo enters. He speaks like Mortimer Snerd, as do all television clowns.*)

GOOFO: Hello, boys and girls. I know that a lot of you are still up at four in the morning, and it's wonderful to look out there and see your sleepy, stupid-looking little faces. This is your old friend, Goofo the Clown, here to tell you exactly what to do. Tiptoe into daddy's and mommy's room right now, kids. That's it. Be sure to take the TV set with you. Be very quiet.

Now you'll see daddy's *pants* over the chair near the bed. Very carefully put your little hand into his pants pocket and take out his wallet. That's the idea. Take out his wallet, open it up very quietly and take out those little green pieces of paper. Take out *all* of them. Let's suppose that there's *ten* of those green pieces of paper in daddy's wallet. Now put *one* of those little green pieces of paper in an envelope and mail it tonight to Prickly Heat, in care of this station. Then take the *other* nine little green pieces of paper with the pictures of George Washington or Abraham Lincoln on them, put them in a *second* envelope and address it personally to Goofo the Clown, in care of Box 27, Grand Central Station, New York.

That's it for now, boys and girls. And remember . . . don't get those envelopes mixed up, or I'll getcha! Good night, kids.

STEVE: Good night, Goofo, and thanks so much for being here tonight. Isn't he a great trouper, folks? And I know that all you little punk—*kids*—are going to do exactly what he said. Whatever it was. I wasn't listening.

Well, that brings us up to the last few minutes of our big annual telethon, ladies and gentlemen. Let's get back to the total board and see how much money has been raised up to this moment. The new total is . . .

Music: Fanfare

One hundred and seven dollars! Listen, I don't mind telling you I'm getting pretty sick of this! You're nothin' but a bunch of cheapskates, you hear me? I've had enough!!

As soon as I go off the air this morning I have to catch a plane to Chicago where I'm MC'ing another telethon—a *great* one—aimed at stamping out the greatest killer of them all . . . *Natural Causes.*

As for this—forget it. You all stink! (*He goes off the air screaming and crying.*)

Music: Playoff

(*Applause*)

THE TAMING OF THE SHREW

STEVE: You know, one of the big motion pictures this year is *The Taming of the Shrew*, starring Richard Burton and Elizabeth Taylor. It's a big, colorful rendition of the play by William Shakespeare. There's an article in this copy of *American Education* (*He is holding magazine*) that says English teachers might recommend the picture to those students who don't seem to be interested in Shakespeare. But I've talked to a few teen-agers who have seen the film, and still have some difficulty with the language.

To solve the problem we've put together a production of *Taming of the Shrew* especially designed for today's high-school students, teeny boppers, dropouts, and whatever.

I'll get into my costume and we'll play the sketch for you right after this message.

(*Commercial*)

Scene: A medieval Italian street scene. Exterior. Torture cage hangs near building. Woman in rags and long black hair kneels penitently in cage. Passersby walk along. A laborer pulls a cart past. Steve and Louie enter on two tame horses. They dismount. Servant takes horses away.

Music: "Green" Middle-ages folk sound. Building into Symphonic mood.

Credits crawl or supered: *Metro-Go-Go-Mayer* presents:

The putting down of the hip shrew, a happening by Willie Shakespeare.

The Scene: Paduasville

Time: Like 1572.

LOUIE: Dear master, hére we are in Padua at last.
　　　　And I must say that by this neighborhood I'm gassed.
　　　　This must be last of all our weary stops.
　　　　I ask you if you think this makes it, pops.

STEVE: Why, yes it does, my friend, both wise and witty.
　　　　In Padua we'll to the nitty-gritty.
　　　　I've come to find a wife on whom to lean
　　　　And that, good sir, is why I've made the scene.

LOUIE: Crazy. (*Beat*) I'm at thy side, my master Pinocchio.

STEVE: That's *Petruchio*, you fool. Pinocchio's the one with
the funny nose.

LOUIE: (*Looks at his face*) I know what I'm talking about,
Slim.

STEVE: Enough, you varlet. You're a churlish fellow,
　　　　But I must find a chick who's yellow mellow.
　　　　So knock, sir, at the door of yonder hall.
　　　　Perchance within its walls we'll have a ball.
　　　　Knock, I say.

LOUIE: Knock, sir? Whom should I knock? I'm just a clown,
　　　　But I'll avenge the man who's put you down.

STEVE: Knock me, I say.

LOUIE: I would not think I'd take the task for it,
　　　　But as for knocking, daddy-o, you asked for it.

(*He walks behind Steve who is looking the other way and belts
him with a club.*)

Sound: Thump of hit on head

STEVE: No, you ignoramus, not my head!
　　　　Pray, knock upon the castle door instead.
　　　　Yea, knock there soundly, roundly; don't mean maybe.
　　　　Draw back thy fist and sock-it-to-me, baby.

LOUIE: But wait, my master, which of all these doors
　　　　Belongs to her who one day will be yours?
　　　　We've the address, so far that isn't bad.
　　　　But which of these is then your true love's pad?

(*Camera shows doors marked with old Italian print* 1A, 2B, 3C.)

I see apartment 1-A listed here.
And yet right next 2-B is printed clear.
Apartment 3-C's printed very big
So which one shall I knock at, if you dig?

STEVE: Methinks it's not 1-A. 2-B? 2-B or not 2-B?
That is the question.
Perhaps the super we should now awaken,
And see if he can hip us to what's shakin'.

LOUIE:
(*He knocks at door. It opens and Dayton Allen appears.*)
(*He does Groucho.*)

STEVE: Ah, it is the father of fair Katherine, whom I am bound to wed.

DAYTON: Say the secret word and you win three hundred lira.
For now my advice is: Don't come any nearer.

STEVE: Good day, kind sir. I'm here to woo your child.
Because I've heard she's really pretty wild.
I seek her hand, fairest from north to south.

DAYTON: Her hand? You'll get it right across the mouth.

STEVE: My name, good sir, Petruchio.
And this, my manservant Lucentio.
Outside you'll find my horse, Pistachio.

DAYTON: My name is Grouchio. And though my hair is balding,
Sometimes I'm also known as Captain Spaulding.

LOUIE: (*He takes Steve aside*) My lord, explain just how this silly wretch
Has any true connection with this sketch?

STEVE: Villain, I say, forget you our rehearsal?
When we, fearing a critical reversal,
Took all the laughs we could and threw them in?
Who cares for sense, if audiences grin?
(*To Dayton*) Well, prithee, sire, wilt give thy daughter up?

113

DAYTON: Yes, stranger, that I wilt, you bet.
    The problem is, *she* hasn't wilted yet.
    Though pretty, she might as well be a hag
    For getting married doesn't seem to be her bag.
    Come in, then, ere your heady passion melts.
    When you meet Kate you'll see she's somethin' else.

STEVE: I know your family not, good friend. Hast thou a coat of arms?

DAYTON: Coat of arms? I don't even have a decent pair of pants!

STEVE: (*He and Louie enter the hall. We see the interior. Camera reveals a large, colorful coat of arms on wall*)
    How, now, good sir, I spy upon the wall
    Your family crest. 'Tis most impressive all.

DAYTON: Yes, that's our *crest* all right, and if you please
    I must say it's reduced our cavities.

LOUIE: Dear Grouchio, my master isn't piggy,
    But can he meet your most tempestuous Twiggy?
    We're at an impasse. I desire to break it.
    Let's find out if these crazy kids can make it.

DAYTON: Well, when she comes be sure she knows who's boss
    Or else that you're protected by Blue Cross.

LOUIE: I warn you, sire, make not my lord a monkey.
    At once, I say, produce this tempting wench.

STEVE: Yes, produce this monkey-wench!
    I know that joke's a relic,
    But this whole bit is somewhat psychodelic.

DAYTON: (*He starts to climb steps to balcony leading to Jayne's room.*)
    And now, Petruchio, I go to fetch fair Kate.
    I still think that your judgment is most faulty;
    She's mighty pretty, but she comes on salty.
    Sound: Glass and furniture breaking. Bumps and thumps

JAYNE: (*Special effects: Crockery and pieces of furniture fly through the now opened door. Two servant ladies run out cower-*

114

ing in terror and descend the steps, looking back fearfully.) No, I won't have it. Get out. Get out, you idiots! Leave me in peace, do you hear!!! I'll skin you alive! I'll cut off your head and throw it in your face! Leave me alone, do you understand! Out! Out!

DAYTON: Ah, wonderful. She's in good spirits today.

JAYNE: (*She enters beating and throwing things at the servants. She swings on chandelier across the stage. This can be stunt woman if necessary. Crashes into wall. Knocks things down, chases women from room. Circles back in through patio door.*)

  Get out, you stupid nincompoops.

  And leave me now in peace.

  If either should return

  I'll boil you in hot grease!

DAYTON: My child, your fiery temper! Can you rule it?

  In any case, I now suggest you cool it.

STEVE: May I present myself, fair lady,

  I am Petruchio, and I am proud and mighty.

JAYNE: You're not my type. You'd better get lost, whitey.

LOUIE: Dear master, this rude witch may test your wit.

STEVE: (*To Jayne*) Now may I have a word with thee—?

JAYNE: Yeah. *Split!*

STEVE: Fair Kate, a sweeter smile there never was.

JAYNE: Jack, get lost, or I'll scream for the fuzz!

STEVE: Lucentio, I put the test to you.

  Would *you* say she's a shrew?

LOUIE: I don't know. She doesn't *look* shrewish.

JAYNE: Oh, no? Well, get a load of this!

(*She starts to hit Steve, with breakaway chairs, bottles, Italian glass jars, etc. Crockery, what-have-you. Dust flies, sound effects and the drummer emphasizes the mayhem.*)

  I want no man at all.

  I'd sooner die than let this pox upon me fall.

(*After a last clout she gets up close to him.*)

  There. What do you think of that?

STEVE: (*A la Ed Sullivan*) You . . . are a shrew.

  A really big shrew.

And next week, on our stage, my little frail
I'll wed thee, and we two will really wail!

LOUIE: Why not now, master, while the iron is hot?
Before it all goes to—you should pardon the
expression—pot.

STEVE: A good idea, Lucentio. Sire, are you prepared
To state at last your daughter has been snared?

DAYTON: Well, I should consult my *attorneys* about this.

STEVE: Attorneys? But why, sir, and who *are* they?

DAYTON: A wonderful firm. Prosciutto and Melon.

JAYNE: No, no. I said it then, I say it now.
I won't be bought and sold like some mere cow.
I won't wed you, you four-eyed drip.
As far as I'm concerned, go take a trip!

STEVE: Enough of this. I've had my fill of sass.
I've stood it, woman, 'cause you *are* a gas!
Good Grouchio, I'm more than man enough for
Kate.
I would that there were *two* of her.

DAYTON: Two of her? Then I'd have Kate and *Duplikate!*
But very well, Petrook, you'll be her mate.
Can't wait to see you boppers do the skate.

JAYNE: I tell you once again, man, that it's *no* go.

STEVE: We'll honeymoon tonight at Whiskey-a-go-go!
Lucentio, you are empowered, are you not
To solemnize a marriage on the spot?
If there be peace with justice, why then please
Do serve us now as justice of the peace.

LOUIE: Dearly beloved, we are gathered here
To wed a cat who would, to one who'd not,
Sire, do you take this woman?

STEVE: Yeah, man. For everything she's got!

LOUIE: Then I declare until death do you part.

DAYTON: This marriage's off to a rotten start.
Congratulations, son. I'll wring your hand, by
heck.
(*They shake hands.*) Kiss him, daughter.

116

JAYNE: I'd rather wring his *neck!*

STEVE: But now, my swinger, our first kiss can wait
    Until I've cooled you to a gentle mate,
    We must away to Pisa, my fair flower,
    If we make haste, we'll make it in an hour.
    Lucentio! My trusty steed, kind sir,
    And bring something to ride, as well, for her.

LOUIE: At once, Petruchio. My service never stops
    I'll get the horses on the double, pops.

(Louie exits. Outside again we see the medieval torture cage with the ragged woman in it. Louie leads in one horse for Steve—very tame—and the white sway-backed one for Jayne: Jayne struggles to get on.)

LOUIE: This used to belong to the White Knight.

STEVE: Yeah. *He* was stronger than dirt, but the horse wasn't.

JAYNE: If ride this nag I must, then,
    Put me up, at once I say.

STEVE: Listen, mama, stop your angry frown.
    I'll put you up; no longer put me down.
    Climb on yourself, my downy little duck;
    If you can't make it, baby, lotsa luck.

LOUIE: *(He has taken a mandolin from saddle bag)*
    Observe how groovily I play for you
    As now this township does the boogaloo.

Music: Rock and roll guitar. Starting as if played by Louie's mandolin, then building right up into strong beat.

(Woman in cage does go-go cage-girl steps, townspeople—dancers —in street do a few hip steps. Fade out. Applause.)

PART TWO

The scene is Petruchio's home. Same general kind of look only rundown; cobwebs, smudges on walls, etc.

Servants stand about. Fireplace. Long table. Steve is at one end of table, surrounded by food. Jayne is at the other end, starving.

JAYNE: Please, I pray you, give me food to eat. Even a crust.

STEVE: You've got a lot of crust already, baby. You're a little overweight as it is. (*He holds carcass of bird. Looks at it. Says:*) Alas, poor Yorick, I knew him well.

> Ran a Chicken Delight joint in San Rafael.

JAYNE: But, sir, I haven't eaten in three days.

STEVE: How can I leave thee? Let me count the ways.

JAYNE: I hunger for a bit, as in a famine.

> I thirst for just one drink as in a drouth.

STEVE: One of these days, pow, right in the mouth.

LOUIE: (*He enters with dessert tray. Cream pies on it.*)
> Ah, master, I have now prepared for thee
> The sweetest, rich dessert you'll ever see.
> Like, it's so groovy, all would call it nice,
> But it's three thousand calories a slice.
> It's fine banana cream. I wasn't lazy.

STEVE: Did you say banana? Jack, that's really crazy.
> Enough of that. What think you one and all
> Of how I've humbled Kate within this hall?

> She came in high and mighty, very proud
> But now in deep humility she's bowed.

(*The servants stand around smiling, nodding.*)
> It goes to show, my friends, we take no chance
> When firmly we make clear who wears the pants.

> The woman knows her place that she's been put
> Why, if I asked it, she would kiss my foot.

JAYNE: (*Rises, moves toward him*)
> Ah, master, I would please you with a kiss,
> But first there, Charlie, get a load of this!

(*She hits him in the face with a pie.*)

STEVE: Thanks. I needed that!

(*He looks into camera. Does take. Wipes cream away.*)
> Fair Kate, I warn you. Do not try to sneak out.
> Because you're askin' for a real freak-out.

Mama, I've underestimated you.

So, it's tit for tat; here comes pie number *two!*

(*He hits* her *in the face with a pie. At each clout the drummer makes a big noise to emphasize the splat.*)

LOUIE: Oh, that is funny! What a silly scrape.

JAYNE: Daddy-o, methinks *you'll* not escape.

(*She hits Louie with a pie.*)

DAYTON: (*He enters*) Good day to all. I've just come from the South.

What's this? My daughter frothing at the mouth?

JAYNE: Pops, you've got an awful lot of nerve!

For marrying me to him, *this* you deserve!

(*She hits Dayton with a pie.*)

DAYTON: I never knew how true it was, all right,

To say (*He wipes eyes*) that you were really out of sight.

STEVE: To think she'd lay one on you really hard.

DAYTON: It's enough to make me want to burn my card.

(*He hits Jayne with pie.*)

Forsooth, Lucentio, your marriage? Doth it go?

STEVE: Forsooth and seven years ago, I know

When you were born, who knew 'twould be the case

Even our viewers would get one in the face?

(*Steve turns to camera which is taking a shot through glass or plastic sheet. Hits sheet with pie, covering screens at home.*)

Music: Rock and roll version of "Keep Telling Me" *up to big finish. Cut back to shot of whole group coming downstage for bows, covered with pie cream.*

Super the words, in medieval type:

Man, this is really—

The End.

SONNY COOL

ANNOUNCER: We are interviewing one of the most influential of today's young musicians, a man equally at home in the fields of pure jazz, rock and roll, folk rock, rock folk, roke fock, and whatever. Here *is* . . . Sonny Cool.

SONNY: That's right. Here I *is*.

ANNOUNCER: Mr. Cool, you are currently appearing in town with the Sonny Cool Sextet. Tell me, who are the members of the sextet?

SONNY: Well, there's like me. And my drummer, Crash Diet. And my flautist, Mohammed Jones.

ANNOUNCER: That's only three people. How about the other four that make up the sextet?

SONNY: Yeah, how about them? They're too much. Actually they rarely show up.

But it's cool, 'cause when we get to their choruses like we just lay out and *think* about what they'd play if they were on the scene, you dig?

ANNOUNCER: I'm not sure. What is *your* instrument, Mr. Cool?

SONNY: I play the ivories.

ANNOUNCER: Ah, you play the piano.

SONNY: No, man. Not the piano. The *ivories*. It's a bunch of elephant tusks laced together.

ANNOUNCER: I see.

SONNY: I doubt it.

It makes a groovy sound, but while you're playin' you got to keep an eye on the *trunk* every inch of the way. It can reach right up and grab you by the klaveman, you know.

ANNOUNCER: How did you happen to form your sextet, Mr. Cool?

SONNY: Well, like I took these young cats and I welded them into a real fine group, you know? I welded them into a fine outfit.

ANNOUNCER: You see yourself then as a band leader?

SONNY: No, as a welder.

ANNOUNCER: What are your hobbies, Sonny?

SONNY: Well, man, like I dig sports cars. In fact I am now driving a crazy set of wheels. Really too much. It's got full pipes, six carburetors, twin gaskets, and does a groovy 125 in second. And now I'm saving up some bread to get some extra equipment for it. Somethin' I've always wanted.

ANNOUNCER: What's that?

SONNY: A steering wheel.

ANNOUNCER: (*He coughs nervously*)

SONNY: What's the matter, man?

ANNOUNCER: I—uh—I think I need a little drink to wet my whistle.

SONNY: What is that shiny little thing you took out of your pocket that you're *drinkin'* out of, man?

ANNOUNCER: That's a hip flask.

SONNY: It don't look so hip to *me*.

ANNOUNCER: Never mind. Listen, you mentioned your flautist. What does a flautist play?

SONNY: He plays the flaut. You puttin' me on?

ANNOUNCER: Well, yes. I put you on about two minutes ago, and we've both been on since then.

SONNY: Crazy. What are *you* on?

ANNOUNCER: On the *air*.

SONNY: Oh, groovy. I'll have to try that. Some sort of a Zen or Yoga scene, I suppose.

ANNOUNCER: I'm afraid I don't follow you.

SONNY: I'd be afraid if you *did*, man.

ANNOUNCER: Tell me, where are you playing in town? At what club?

SONNY: Last week we played at a place called Far In. Now we're at a place called Somethin' Else.

ANNOUNCER: And what else is it called?

SONNY: What else is *what* called?

ANNOUNCER: The place you're playing.

SONNY: I just told you. It's Somethin' Else.

ANNOUNCER: Never mind. Tell me, what songs are you recording at present?

SONNY: Well, like I just did an album called "Sonny With Strings."

ANNOUNCER: You used violins?

SONNY: No, man. Strings. You know, like twine, thread, skinny rope. You can get groovy sounds outta them little mothers if you pluck 'em just right, you dig? But I recorded some nice old tunes, some mood things.

ANNOUNCER: Such as?

SONNY: Such as Stokely Carmichael's "Star Dust."

ANNOUNCER: I see. Mr. Cool, you have a lot of young fans who wear strange clothes and live by their own rules. What do you think of boys with hair longer than their girl friends?

SONNY: With hair longer than their girl friends' what?

ANNOUNCER: I don't know. I must say that I don't seem to be doing a very good job of uncovering the real inner Sonny Cool. I wonder what makes you tick?

SONNY: I don't know, man, unless it's this cheap wristwatch I'm wearing. But don't worry, pops. After all, we just met.

ANNOUNCER: Not really. You see, you literally bumped into me at the airport here in town about six weeks ago.

SONNY: Oh, well, excuse me, man.

Sorry I took so long to apologize.

ANNOUNCER: It's nothing. Mr. Cool, you're also a composer of music. Just how do you write your songs?

SONNY: Brilliantly.

ANNOUNCER: I see. Well, one last question. What would you say to young people who want to follow in your footsteps?

SONNY: If they find anything I dropped I hope they'll bring it to me before the fuzz finds it.

But, seriously, I think young cats who want to make the scene should form a group and get a good name for themselves.

ANNOUNCER: How do you mean . . . get a good name?

SONNY: You know, like The Electric Prunes . . . The Chocolate Watchband . . . The Jefferson Airplane . . . The Lincoln Tunnel. In fact, I invented a name machine that can make up names all by itself.

ANNOUNCER: How does it work?

SONNY: Well, it's got two sections, see. One section is full of adjectives, like *chocolate, electric, yellow, velvet, sideways,* and so forth. Then the other section is full of nouns. Like *watchband, apple sauce, sweatshirt, hockey puck*, you dig?

Now you just take a word from column A, and a word from column B, and you automatically got the name of a new group. Look, here. We shake up the box and we got *The Chocolate Catcher's Mitt, The Electric Jockstrap.*

ANNOUNCER: I see. And The Velvet Garbage Can.

SONNY: And The Peanut Butter Brassiere.

ANNOUNCER: And The Oatmeal Typewriter.

SONNY: The Molasses Draft Card.

ANNOUNCER: The Presbyterian Glove-compartment.

SONNY: The Lead Truss.

They gradually are faded out.

MR. KNOW-IT-ALL (FOR LAUGH-IN, JULY 31, 1972)

DAN: Ladies and gentlemen, we're very honored to have with us this evening a man who just happens to be an *expert*, on almost *any* subject you could name. Whether your questions are about *politics, science, philosophy—whatever—*this man can answer them.

Music: "The Miracle of America"

DICK: Hello, Mr. Know-it-all. It's nice to *have* you here.

STEVE: Thank you, Mr. Martin, and may I say that it's nice to be *had*.

DAN: Well, Mr. Know-it-all, we have some very interesting questions tonight. Would you mind if we put them *to* you?

STEVE: It will get awfully quiet out here if you *don't*.

DAN: The first question, which comes from someone in our audience, is: What's the best way to hear about a good *orthodontist.*

STEVE: By word of mouth.

DAN: Mr. Know-it-all, in the theatre of international conflict, who would you say are *the greatest Western leaders* of our time?

STEVE: Greatest Western leaders? Well, one of the first of them I would say was Hopalong Cassidy. Then there was Tom Mix, Hoot Gibson, Gene Autry and John Wayne. In that order.

DICK: Next question, Mr. Know-it-all. Is *plastic surgery* really effective? And is it expensive?

STEVE: Certainly, it's effective. I just went to a great plastic surgeon. He gave me a new *nose* and a new *chin*.

DAN: Was he very *expensive?*

STEVE: He charged me an arm and a leg.

DICK: The next question, Mr. Know-it-all, is extremely interesting. A lady in our audience asks, "What can you tell us about *Cloris Leachman?*"

STEVE: Well, I'll say this. Cloris Leachman is the basic ingredient in most of your standard washday detergents.

Cloris Leachman is so effective that it will make even your *colored* clothes come out *sparkling white!*

DAN: Mr. Know-it-all, here's a timely question. Are modern automobile tires—the ones made with *polyglass*—really *safe?*

STEVE: Oh, yes. They're at the very least as safe as any other. Although just the other day, I did get a *flat* in one of my polyglass tires.

DICK: How did that happen?

STEVE: I ran over a piece of *rubber.*

DICK: Mr. Know-it-all, what do you think would be the proper solution for the problem of campus unrest?

STEVE: Campus unrest? I would say put some nice soft mattresses all over the dormitories. You can't get a good rest with those hard mattresses.

DAN: Mr. Know-it-all, what do you think of the *Sino-Soviet situation?*

STEVE: I have every confidence that the Sino-Soviet situation will work out just fine. That was my conclusion on the basis of my recent visit to the Soviet. However, I admit that I have never been to Sino.

DICK: Mr. Know-it-all, here's a question from a *sports fan.* We hear a lot about Joe Namath's "trick knee." What does that expression *mean,* "trick knee?"

STEVE: It means just what it says. Joe's left knee can do lots of tricks. I personally have seen it do a *somersault*. I've also seen it *go fetch the paper*. I have seen it *roll over and play dead*.

DICK: Mr. Know-it-all, is it true that you personally went to college in Arizona?

STEVE: Yes, I went to Arizona State Teachers' College.

DAN: Arizona? What did you *major* in?

STEVE: I majored in Tumbleweed. My electives were *Moseying* and *Sagebrush*. And I took my master's in *Ornery Sidewinders*.

DAN: Here's a question, sir, from a school teacher in our audience. She has a friend who says she's *quadrilingual*. What does that mean, "quadrilingual?"

STEVE: I knew a woman once who was quadrilingual. She spoke only one language, but she had *four tongues*. When she talked it was a *terrible* sight.

DAN: Get off the stage, Mr. Know-it-all!

THE ROLLICKING GOURMET

JAYNE: Good morning again. I know that you ladies *particularly* will be *thrilled* to hear that we have with us in our Los Angeles studio this morning that charming man from down under . . .

STEVE: (*His head rises into a medium shot, from the bottom of the picture.*)
Good morning. I've just been *down under* there and I was . . .

JAYNE: Oh! You startled me, sir.

Anyway, ladies, here *is* that adorable, irrepressible and oh-so-witty visitor from Australia—the Rollicking Gourmet, Mr. Graham Cracker.

Good morning, Mr. Cracker.

STEVE: Good morning, Miss Meadows.

JAYNE: We're so *delighted* to have you with us.

STEVE: Well, I've been looking forward to it. My sister *Saltine* was on the program recently and she told me how very much she enjoyed it.

JAYNE: Well, we just have a couple of minutes, Mr. Cracker. What recipe would you like to show us today?

STEVE: Well, today we're going to cook ourselves *silly*, aren't we?

First of all, I think every woman ought to know how to make good, rich soup.

You start, needless to say, with a good beef stock. I personally have selected Armour's Preferred, which closed yesterday at 45 and a half (*As he says this he cuts up a gilt-edged share of stock into little pieces and drops them into a pot.*)

Now it just so happens that I have a perfectly marvelous recipe for good, rich *soup*. And here it is. (*He lifts up an old tire on which the word "Goodrich" is printed.*)

First you cut up a Goodrich tire, into small pieces, remembering, of course, to remove the inner tube. But more about that later. (*He throws tire aside.*)

And now here's a little something special from *down under*. Down under the table. (*He reaches down, takes a belt of wine from a bottle and throws some into the pot.*)

I know what you're thinking. I didn't start the show with my usual witty story, from the bar. Very well. (*He seats himself on a bar stool at bar stage right.*)

Well, it seems these two Jews got off a streetcar in Sydney. Or no . . . *Sidney* got off a streetcar in Jerusalem. So one of them said to the other (*Irish accent*), "Tell me, Pat, how come Father O'Brien doesn't hear your confession any more?"

And the *other* Greek said . . . or no, the old *woman* said to the man with the saxophone, "That's an ill woodwind that nobody blows good."

(*He laughs hysterically at his own joke.*)

Now of course there's the question of *dessert*.

How about a nice *mince pie*?

First you require a *greased pan*. (*One is handed in.*) Thank you, Stuart. And you've got a pretty greasy pan yourself.

Next you *fold an egg* into your batter. (*He takes a rubber "fried egg" and folds it in half.*)

126

You can fold your egg *this way* . . . or *that* way, for all of me. (*Sings*) "All of me . . ."

But into the flour it goes.

Next we take a nice green *quince* and *mince* it. I've always wanted to mince a quince. Or . . . if you don't *mince* it . . . you can *dice* it. (*He cuts up two little dice and starts to shoot craps with them.*)

Come on, dice! Baby needs a pair of shoes!

If you change your mind in midstream, as it were, as you were, Stuart, why, you may add all these ingredients into one and make a *paella*. If you are Spanish you pronounce it *pie-ayah*. Otherwise *pie-ella*. I mix it with an old Scottish recipe from the Fitzgerald Clan so that we can end up with a *Pie Ella Fitzgerald*.

So we add the *quince*, the rubber *tire*, the *egg*, the *flour* and the *beef stock* into the large bowl.

If you're writing these ingredients down, remember: the meat of a *quince*, the juice of a *lemon*, the yolk of an *egg*, the eye of an *eagle*, the heart of a *lion*, the hand of a *woman*, the wisdom of a *Solomon*, and these are the qualities of a good *physician*.

Well, I see by the old clock on the wall that we need a *new* clock on the wall, so until lunchtime tomorrow, this is your galloping, rollicking, toddling, tripping, trotting, traipsing, gamboling gourmet, Graham Cracker saying, "Ta-Ta!"

Chapter Four

TELEVISION MONOLOGUES

I have often thought that after twenty years of talk show prattle the art of conversation is in danger of being lost altogether. The point is not that important issues fail to be discussed. Some hosts can make any important issue seem unimportant—but there is a general failure to create dialogue on the Talk Show. Even less creative is the usual talk show monologue. To sit and talk when there is someone there to help is difficult enough, but to stand up and do it alone requires consummate skill, though not having it doesn't seem to deter many. To acquire a perfect sense of timing, to achieve rapport with an audience, to communicate fully with body language, and in addition to have something funny to say and to say it in a witty way requires a magic gift. Most talk show hosts simply lack that magic. It is not to say they do not have attractive personalities and a certain type of talent, but usually they do not have that specific ability, nor the training which leads to it. When they rise to do a comedy monologue, obviously the real comedian has not stood up. Johnny Carson and Steve Allen seem the only exceptions.

Steve Allen invited me to dinner, but I couldn't join him because Merv Griffin was suddenly taken ill. What Griffin's flu had to do with my not having dinner at Steve Allen's is that Allen was called at the last minute to serve as guest host. He graciously invited me to view the show, which provided an opportunity to observe at firsthand his magnetic hold of an audience. Although the Hollywood Palace is a large theatre he had the audience in the palm of his hand, a task not made easier by the fact that the visitors had come especially to see Griffin.

Perhaps the greatest accomplishment of an entertainer is to take a large impersonal audience and at once create a personal atmosphere. And that's exactly what Steve accomplished. Although he had almost no advance notice, his monologue was entirely polished and delivered as if a stock routine. Every gesture, every grimace, every movement were perfectly orchestrated to produce the appropriate humorous effect, and a very funny line of thought was developed:

You're probably wondering where Merv is. I know *I* am. Well, Merv was in a hot poker game last night, and he lost the show.
No, Merv came down with the bug—that's something you get from watching Watergate.
But the *real* story is that it's Merv's mother's birthday, and so he had to go to San Quentin to visit her.
No, seriously, I'm filling in for Merv because he had a slight accident—I ran over him.
Actually, Merv is sick, but game trouper he is . . . Did you know Merv was once a *game* trooper?

In the meantime, Allen had been fooling around with his right ear. He kept shaking his head and complaining the ear would not open. Being actually bothered with the ear he did an eccentric kind of walk, and quipped, "Now I know why Cary Grant walked like this."

The funny stream of jokes was somehow perfectly complemented by the irrelevant business with the ear.

What is noteworthy about Allen's routines is that he doesn't just throw out one-liners unrelated, Bob Hope style, but creates a comic situation, which requires a far more inventive capacity. In the summer of 1972, when Steve Allen did a week as guest host on the Dick Cavett show, Gerald Nachman wrote in the New York *Daily News* that "If this were the best of possible worlds, Steve Allen would be hosting his own show in New York instead of just taking over this week for Dick Cavett. . . ." Mr. Nachman is saying Allen is the best at what he does.

Comedy has an anarchistic strain; it works by making fun of all things. Since power must be taken seriously to maintain itself, comedy is always a threat to it. In our age when power has the potential of becoming absolute, the realm of humor may be a last refuge for freedom. For humor may be the last truly effective way for man to resist the immense gravitational field of authority pulling him down. By laughing at power comedy says "no" to its tyrannical demands.

Because comedy has a negative function it should not surprise us to discover a number of negative comedians about. Such comedians work off their anger in a positive way by attacking absurdity in the world. Steve Allen is not an angry comedian, but in his good-natured way he shows us this is not the best of all possible worlds. In fact, he makes us see it does not even work very well. On the "Tonight Show," with Rich Little as guest host, Steve observed we were able to send a man to the moon but that here on earth the country was coming apart at the edges. Things just do not seem to work any more and everywhere things, little and big, go wrong. We have *rockets* to the heavens but you can no longer expect a limousine to meet you at an airport. When Steve came to Chicago, a woman assigned to meet him, having heard of his misgivings about limousines, was determined she would get him one. It never arrived, of course.

Still determined to provide Steve with transportation from the airport, she brought her own car and parked it in a convenient spot—unfortunately also a "no parking" area, from which the car was quickly towed away. Steve told her not to worry; they could just hop in a cab. Unfortunately there was none around to hop into. They had to wait an hour. Finally, when they got a cab, the cabbie refused to put the luggage in the trunk. Steve couldn't understand why, and the driver explained there was a company rule against putting luggage in the luggage compartment. With that Steve snapped, "Put it in the glove compartment, and let's go."

As Steve Allen recounted the true story it was delightfully funny. Most people consider such experiences painfully disturbing. The humorist, however, creates a new orientation and transforms the world of woe.

From the foibles of man Steve Allen develops some hilarious situations in the monologues which follow:

THE TRUTH ABOUT THE GREAT INVENTORS

I have a theory that famous American inventors—Thomas Edison, Eli Whitney and the rest of them—really have gotten more credit than they deserve. I'm not knocking the cotton gin or the phonograph, mind you. What I object to is that there is implicit in the lavish praise heaped upon our prominent inventors the assumption that practically everything they ever turned their hands to was a success. This just wasn't the case. You've heard about the big hits and successes these inventors had, but you've been told practically nothing about their flops.

Certainly Alexander Graham Bell invented the telephone. Good for him. But he also invented the talking wastebasket. And he wasted years working on a battery-operated suit of long underwear.

Tom Edison invented the phonograph. A wonderful achievement, I admit. But have you ever noticed the picture of that dog sitting in front of one of the early models of his machine? That's the tipoff. You and I now use that appliance for playing records. But as far as Edison was concerned, it was just a device for calling dogs.

And at that he had to smear the loudspeaker with gravy to really pull them in from any distance.

Eli Whitney invented the cotton gin. OK, great. But look at

all his bombs. He also invented the *wool* gin; a terrible fiasco. Killed thousands of sheep. And very painfully, too.

And even his first model of the cotton gin was no good. It saved the seeds and threw the cotton away.

Then take Robert Fulton, the man who invented the steamboat. He also invented the fish market, although not many people know about that. So all right, he deserves credit for the two accomplishments. But he, too, had a long series of failures with other devices driven by steam. He invented the steam typewriter. (Burned your fingers; soggy paper.) The steam lawnmower. (Burned the grass to a frazzle.) The steam toothbrush. (Very rough on the gums.) Although I'll admit the teeth were mighty clean when they fell out.

Then look at the Wright Brothers. A couple of real phonies. Contrary to what you were told in schoolbooks, they did not invent the airplane. That thing was a propeller-driven boat they were putting together. With two outriggers.

Haven't you ever wondered why they went to the *beach* at Kitty Hawk to try it out? They were just trying to push the thing downhill into the water to find out if it would float. Wilbur happened to say, "Listen, Orville, maybe if you just *sat* in it to keep it from blowing up in the air all the time. . . ."

So they turned on the propeller and the breeze caught the outriggers and the damned thing lifted up into the air.

They were both terribly embarrassed.

WHAT ELSE DID THEY SAY?

Everyone is familiar with certain remarks made by historical figures, remarks which, for one reason or another, have been recorded in the annals of history. It is remarkable, I think, that— although a man may have spent forty or fifty years in public life —during which time he presumably said thousands of important things, nevertheless it is often only *one single sentence* that comes down through the ages to us.

Did you ever wonder what these great men said immediately *after* their so-well-remembered remarks? Well, I have checked into the matter and I can bring you some of my findings at this time.

Remember the great sea battle when the British commander said to John Paul Jones, "Are you prepared to strike your colors, sir?" and Jones said, "I have not yet begun to fight."

Do you know the very next thing he said? He said, "And I ain't about to begin to fight. You can get *killed* out here."

And of course you all know that Patrick Henry said "Give me liberty or give me death." But you've never been told his *complete* statement. It went like this, "Give me liberty or give me death; preferably in that order."

And we are told in the Scriptures that at the beginning of time the Lord said, "Let there be light." But I've checked this out with a number of eminent biblical scholars. The Lord's *complete* statement was as follows: "Let there be light. Well, maybe not *all* day."

Everyone, I think, remembers Voltaire's famous line about freedom of speech. The version of it that you are familiar with is actually based on a faulty translation. What Voltaire actually said was this: "I do not agree with what you say, sir, though I will defend to the death your right to say it. But for now . . . shut up!"

And remember the historic moment when the inventor of the telegraph, Samuel Morse, sent his first message. You know he said: "What hath God wrought?"

The very next thing he said was "I *thertainly* wish I knew."

HURRAH FOR MITCHELL PARRISH

You know who wrote "Star Dust"? Hoagy Carmichael? Sure, that's what everybody says. And they're right. But Hoagy only wrote the music. Fellow named Mitchell Parrish wrote the words.

I was arguing with a friend of mine the other day. He said "Star Dust is such a beautiful melody it would have been a hit no matter what words they put to it." I guess a lot of people feel the same way. But it's not so. I'll prove it to you. I just wrote a lyric to "Star Dust" myself. Same title. "Star Dust." But see if you think the song would be as big a hit with *these* words.

STAR DUST

You threw that star dust right at me,
 Right in my face.
Threw it every place.
 I shut my eyes
What a sweet surprise.
 I couldn't see a thing at all.
  All those dusty stars
  Weren't twinkling in the sky there.
  A handkerchief you took
  And dusted all of them there
  And then you shook
  It out on me.
 Oh, gee . . . it's kinda hard to see
 With all that dust,
 Sticking in my eyes.
 Some other guys
 Tried to put me wise.
 But I was blinded by your lies.
  So I wipe it off
  'Cause it kinda makes me want to cough,
 That star dust that you threw
 All over me to make me blue.

THE BIG CONTEST

I was just telling Yves Montand about another American custom that is so popular here—the contest. In magazines and newspapers, on television, and over radio, somebody always seems to be giving something away. We've become so conditioned to this that people often send in box tops even before a contest is announced.

Tonight, to enlighten those of you who haven't entered a contest lately, I am happy to announce. (*Trumpet: Fanfare*) A brand new contest. (*Fanfare*) With fabulous prizes. There's nothing to buy. (*Fanfare*) Nothing to save. (*Fanfare*) And anyone may enter. (*Fanfare*) Except that lousy trumpet player.

Yes, friends, here's the chance of a lifetime in a contest that's easy, fun and exciting. Now, here's all you have to do:

(*A beautiful girl in brief costume brings in easel.*)

Thank you, Darlene. Folks, this is Darlene. I won her in another contest. And I can't even *tell* you what first prize was! Now here are the rules:

First, you must finish the following sentence in ten words or less—

(*Darlene uncovers card ♯1.*)

"I like Darlene because . . ." Now, that's simple, isn't it? Put on your thinking caps and go to work. Thank you, Darlene.

(*She goes.*)

Folks, I'm over here.

Now, when you've finished the sentence, *don't* mail it. There are postal laws, you know. Just hold on to it, because, starting September 30th, 1976, we will publish six photos daily, in the Los Angeles *Mirror*,* which will come as a big shock to Norman Chandler. Now, this is important: These photos have *nothing* to do with this contest. But more about that later.

(*Uncovers card ♯2.*)

On this card are forty-three numbers. Each of these numbers corresponds to a bone in your body. And if you break any of our contest rules, we'll break your bones. But more about that later.

Copy these numbers down on a sheet of paper. Cut them out, and paste them on *another* sheet of paper so that they add up to *zero* in any direction. If you get them to do that, you're *not* following the contest rules.

Next, our special "Look-Alike" feature. We have a special prize for the first one hundred contestants who look like this man:

(*Uncovers card ♯3.*)

(*Hitler*)

They will be flown to New York and publicly humiliated on

---

* The *Mirror* had gone out of business several years earlier.

"Candid Camera!" They will also spend two glorious weeks in the men's room of the Roxy Theatre! And the three top winners will spend a week in my dressing room.

All you do is tell us what famous product uses the following slogan: "Say, men. Are your teeth dingy, dirty and discolored? Well, then keep your mouth shut!"

Next, the official entry blank. If you get one of these entry blanks you're immediately disqualified because this is the *only* one there is. That's a trap we've set for you. But more about that later.

Now, for the *prizes*. And what prizes they are! If you're the winner you'll spend two carefree weeks in a beautiful traffic jam, in the car of your own choice. And that's not all. There are fabulous *cash* prizes, too! But more about that later.

Remember, all entries will be judged on neatness, originality, aptness of thought, and in case of a tie, wear a four-in-hand.

The contest closes in exactly thirty seconds.

The End

THE EX-LUFTWAFFE PILOT

I travel a great deal to other parts of the world; naturally much of this travel is done by airplane. In the United States our pilots all seem cut from the same cloth. They all look like John Wayne or Robert Stack. A few of the older ones look like George Brent, but at least they're the kind of men in whom you instinctively have confidence.

In other parts of the world, however, things are different. The airlines may use secondhand American planes, and goodness knows where they get their pilots from.

I read the other day that several men who are now flying for various small airlines in South America got their early experience under the command of Hermann Goering, in the German Luftwaffe, during World War Two. I was wondering what such a pilot might say to the passengers over the intercom just before take-off, if he were hired by an American airline.

He might sound something like this:

Achtung! Guten morgen, ladies and gentleman. This is Captain Schultz speaking.

First of all I vould like to say . . . no hard feelings!

Our flight today from Los Angeles to New York vill take us over Las Vegas, Nevada—that center of decadence—over the nuclear weapons manufacturing plants at Alamogordo, New Mexico. You vill take no aerial photographs of these facilities whatsoever!

Failure to observe zese instruction vill result in the confiscation of your camera.

Your hostesses on this flight will be Miss Jones, Miss Kelvin, und Miss Rosenberg.

Miss Rosenberg will be vorking in ze back of ze plane.

Shortly after take-off these young ladies will pass among you serving refreshments. You may select coffee, tea or beer.

Please observe the location of your oxygen equipment. Should the pressure in the cabin be reduced below the proper level, an oxygen mask will fall from the panel directly overhead, injuring you severely, if you are not careful.

Since our trip vill take five hours, perhaps some of you may vish to break the monotony by making a brief visit to ze pilots' cockpit to see me fly the plane. Und remember, vhile you are observing me, I vill be observing you.

After refreshments have been served ve vill, of course, be showing a motion picture. The picture today is *The Story of Verner Von Braun*. You vill enjoy particularly the first scene showing Verner as a small schoolboy, already vorking on his rocket experiments. His mother says to him, "Verner, you are a bad boy. You missed school again today." Und Verner says, "Yes, Mama, but zis time only by five hundred yards."*

Passengers vill now fasten their seat belts. That is an order!

Our take-off time is right on schedule at nine twenty-seven und five hours from now ve vill be strafing—er, *landing* at New York.

* A joke for which I am indebted to Bill Dana.

For those of you who like to read, propaganda is available for you in the magazine racks.

There is a hostess call button over your seat, but please, do not make a pest of yourself.

Und now ve haff been cleared for take-off by ze high command. So settle back, relax . . . und . . . . Sig Heil!

HEALTH LECTURE

During the last several years, people have become more and more concerned with what they eat. Nutritionists have written such books as: *Eat for Health, You and Your Heart, You and Your Liver, You and Your Big Mouth, You Are What You Eat,* by Chaz Chase,* *All That Meat and No Potatoes,* and many others.

Well, tonight we have a man who is a real nutrition pioneer. He now comes to us with the latest up-to-the-minute method to get your vitamins and minerals nature's way. Here he is, Dr. Gaylord Allen.

(*Slowly pan up to Steve Allen who is in a cutaway, carrying a large book and wearing pince-nez glasses. A glass of water is on podium.*)

STEVE: Good evening, ladies and gentlemen and eating fans everywhere. I've studied good eating and health for years. And I feel wonderful. I ask you: How long has it been since you leaped out of bed? Well, I did so this morning. (*Holds up leg in large cast.*)

I'm so glad you are able to attend this lecture. I have been lecturing for the past thirty, or is it twelve years?

And I've always said that health is important. Health is healthy and when someone is healthy you have actual healthiness. Remember my words, "Show me a man who is healthy, and I'll show you a man who isn't sick."

But I've made discoveries, and I put these discoveries to work.

---

* A vaudeville pantomimist whose act consisted of eating his boutonniere, his cigarettes, matches, shirt front, hat, etc.

139

I've made countless visits to people who had bad vision. I've talked to a group of people who have been wearing glasses for twenty-four years. I've told them what food to eat. After three months under my care, out of the fifty people who attended, there was not one case of throat irritation.

The human system needs plenty of roughage to facilitate good digestion. Some people get their roughage from things like *bran* and *oatmeal*; I get mine by carrying half a roll of unwrapped cherry Life-Savers in my pocket for about a week. You'd be surprised how much good, rough, pocket lint a cherry Life-Saver can pick up in just seven days. Greatest roughage in the world.

Today people are eating too much. That is all they do, eat, eat, eat. The food today is too soft. The human body, as we know it today is not made for this type of food. You've got to eat more peach pits, cuttle bone and birdseed!

The *cave* man never had to worry about food. They always ate what they could find: roots, grass, raw, uncooked, hard, tough meat. And they did this because they were strong, because they were healthy, and because they were *stupid*.

I believe that with the proper will power you can actually do away with most food. For the past week or so I have done away with most food. I let my body supply its own food. I've not eaten a thing for a week. And I want to state right here and now that . . . (*He falls to the floor and passes out.*)

MONOLOGUE FOR DICK CAVETT SHOW

Hi. This is sort of a difficult theatre to work in. Out in California, the seating in the theatres is horizontal, but in this theatre, seating is more or less vertical. You people way up in the rafters look like bats.
Those *are* bats up there!
Dick's on vacation for a few days.
So am I, come to think of it.
So I thought I'd spend my vacation here on his show.
It's a nice place to vacation. It's quiet here.

Say, did you read in the paper about Jack Paar coming out of retirement? He'll host this show for one week a month. The other three weeks he'll go back into retirement.

You know, Jack made an emotional plea to the network to keep Dick Cavett on the air. Then ABC said, "Do you want Cavett's job?" Jack said, "Yeah, sure, sure!"

I see where the Conservatives in New York are angrier than ever about the welfare mess. They want to change the name of Welfare Island to Lazy-bum Island.

I see here where the Yankees just finished a series with the Milwaukee Brewers. This may date me, but I loved the old team names like Yankees, Giants, Tigers. They really sounded like baseball. But the new names have a terribly commercial ring to them. Like Houston Oilers . . . Milwaukee Brewers.

If that's the way it's going to be, they should rename all the old teams so that the names correspond to the image of the city.

For example, "Well, the Chicago Gangsters beat the Boston Stranglers today."

And on the International sports scene: "The Paris Peace Talkers won a close one over the Philadelphia Cream Cheesers."

I see here where a *Woman's Lib group* is very angry that hurricanes are still being named after *women*, such as *Hurricane Agnes*.

I don't care if they call a storm *Fido*, but I do think it would sound kind of odd to hear a weather man say, "Well, Florida was hit by *Hurricane Gus* this morning. Meanwhile, off the Bahamas, Tropical Storm *Irving* is building up."

Oh, I just got this note from ABC. They have just checked and our rating right now is 6.4. They say if we don't get it up to a 9 by *twelve-thirty*, the last half hour of the show will be *canceled*.

And Jack Paar will do five minutes of it.

FROM HIGH ATOP . . . (The Dance-Band Remote)

You know, when I was a kid growing up it was a time of great music. All the big bands of the thirties and forties were on the radio almost every night. Benny Goodman, Glenn Miller, Glen Gray, Fletcher Henderson.

But even more common were the lesser-known bands that used to play from ballrooms around the country.

Remember the bands that used to play at the old Aragon Ballroom in Chicago?

And the Trianon?

Bands like Anson Weeks and Frankie Masters and Kay Kyser?

Well, it always seemed to me that the same *announcer introduced* all those old orchestras.

And he always sounded something like *this.*

Music: Sammy Kaye Style Introduction—"Last Night I Saw You."
STEVE: Good evening, ladies and gentlemen out there along the radio airwaves.

Music: Band out. Piano alone noodles softly, 1930's style.

From the beautiful Pork Sausage Room, high atop the Jimmy Dean Hotel, in the heart of downtown Cleveland, California—just a short forty-five-minute drive from the ball-bearing center of the world, Leavenworth, Kansas—the National Broadcasing Company is sending your way the rancid rhythms of Jan Savitt and his All-girl Orchestra.

Yes, direct from the stunning new Hump Room of the Camel Motel—built with a nineteen-million-dollar loan from the Central States pension fund—a refreshing two-and-one-half-mile swim across Lake Mishigas, where the Ohio River meets the Panama Canal to form the St. Lawrence Seaway, it's the music of Guy Lombago and the Pennsylvanians with another seventeen solid hours of melodies for your dining and dancing pleasure.

And now, Fletcher and the band support lovely Wamsutta Percale, who is three-sheets-to-the-wind, as she sings the song that this week is number 347 on your Hit Parade, "Smarty Pants."

Music: "Smarty Pants."

SMARTY PANTS

Smarty Pants,
You're such a touchy little Smarty Pants.

There's nothin' you don't know
About romance,
Smarty Pants.
You think you know it all
Be careful or you'll blow it all.

You're such a brain
You give me such a pain
With that old song and dance.
Girls don't like you;
That big I.Q.
Won't get you romance.
Hey, big thinker
You're a fink, ya
Rotten Smarty Pants.

STEVE: Thank you, dear, that was sickening.

Friends, in case you're just joining our jerky jamboree, the Mutual Bumrushing Company is heaving your way the hair-curling music of Henry Kissinger and his *Twelve Angry Men*, direct from the glamorous new Men's Room of the beautiful Edison Hotel, just a short haul from the mouth-watering fig fields of the 1934 Mississippi State Fair Grounds, on the banks of Lake Meshugena, right next door to the lovely Strangler Room on the Boston Turnpike.

Now Woody and the Woodchoppers cold-turkey it up as our swooning, crooning Pillsbury Dough-boy Lyle Socks sings this great standard of 1937, "When There's Stardust on the Moonglow at Sundown Way Down South." Lyle!

Music: Boy or Steve sings "When There's Stardust on the Moonglow."

When there's stardust on the moonglow
at sundown way down South.
Through the tulips
we'll sip juleps
as I try to hush my mouth.

143

There's a rainbow over
a four-leaf clover
when I'm in my mammy's arms.
There's a small hotel
with a wishing well
and I'm dazzled by your charms.

STEVE: Ah, yes, isn't he wonderful, and girls, he's available, because he's just been fired.

Friends, in case you're just tuning in, the Crumbling Block-busting System is unloading its musical trash basket all over you as we present the brain-numbing selections of little Patty Hearst and her Symbionese Swingers, direct from the breath-taking new Powder Room of the Hotel Lastfogel on the outskirts of the Forbidden City, Beverly Hills, California, just a thrilling ten-second rocket flight from the chicken-plucking center of the great Northwest, Capetown, South Africa, Yowsah.

When you come in ask for the à la carte dinner special—Chicken Tetrachloride—prepared by Chef Bivona. You'll recognize the chef; he's the one in the kitchen wearing the Sergeant's flea collar.

But now turn up your radio, roll up the rugs, and plug up your ears as we listen to that lousy little lady of song, Jaynie Ferman singing "I Can't Forget That You've Forgotten Me."
Music: Girl or Jayne sings "Forgetting"

FORGETTING

I can't forget
That you've forgotten me.
Please don't forget
That I forgot
To forget you.

You forgot
That I forgot
To forget
The night we met.

144

I forgot
You were so pettable
It was all so unforgettable.
We can't forget
What we forgot before.
And when forgetting
Is forgotten
Once more.
If your heart forgets
Well, let it.
If you've forgotten me . . .

STEVE: Forget it!
JAYNE: But I haven't *finished* yet.
STEVE: That's what you think, sister!
STEVE: Ah, yes, isn't she lovely? But it's *not definite*.

Friends, if you're tuning in late, the American Back-breaking System is shoving down your throats the sweetest music this side of Sodom and Gomorrah, played by Les Band and His Brown of Renown, direct from the breath-taking new Kung Fu Room of Butte, Montana's own Y.M.C.A. Hotel, underneath McDonald's Golden Arches, where Route 57 meets the Ho Chi Minh Trail to form Key Biscayne; yowsah!

So turn up your radio, roll up the rugs, plug up your ears, and listen to lovely Bob Eberle as he sings a very touching love-song to his dentist, "I Saw You Last Night and Got That Gold Filling":
Music: "That Old Feeling"

I saw you last night
And got that gold filling.
When you fixed my bite
I got that gold filling.

The moment you sat me down
I saw that drill

145

And when you turned it on
It made me ill.

So . . . I saw you last night
And got that gold filling
'Cause it wasn't tight
I'd lost my old filling.
There'll be no newer cavities,
To tell you the truth,
'Cause that gold filling
Is still in my tooth.

STEVE: Ah, yes, friends. He wants to sing in the worst way. And that's just the way he does it.

And of course that was the orchestra's tribute to the great King of Swing himself, Benito Mussolini. And it's all been coming your way from the freshly repainted Roto-Rooter Room of the Tidy-Bowl Motel, halfway between the Firestone Tire Factory and the East St. Louis rendering plant—where the rubber meets the blubber. Yes, indeedy.

To get there you just take the Purgatory off-ramp and drive like hell!

Music: Theme "Last Night I Saw You" (up and under)

But now friends, the Old Clock on the Wall says our *Saturday Night Dancing Party* is on its last legs, so until next time, this is your announcer, Mike Side, mike-side, saying toodle-oo, a bit of a tweet-tweet, a fond adieu, a yock-she-mosh, a bit of a pip-pip, a punch in the mouth, pleasant dreams, an au revoir, an auf Wiederzsehen, good night, good-bye, lots of health, lots of fun, and lotsa luck.

This is NBC, The National Brainwashing Company.

Music: "Last Night I Saw You" *Up to finish.*

Chapter Five

SKETCHES FOR THE THEATRE

Speaking of Dr. Mackenzie King, Mrs. Smith says:

. . . He never prescribes any medicine that he's not tried out on himself first. Before operating on Parker, he had his own liver operated on first, although he was not the least bit ill.

Mr. Smith believed it wrong that the doctor pulled through while the patient died, and he explained that since a captain goes down with his ship a good doctor should go down with his patient. The conclusion was reached that all doctors are quacks and so are all patients, and only the Royal Navy is honest. And another thing, in the papers they always give the age of those who die, but never those who are born.

No, the above madness is not from the Marx Brothers but from the avant-garde playwright Eugene Ionesco. Ionesco believed that the hollow phrases, the meaningless babble, and the clichés and slogans of everyday life were making human communication impossible. Ionesco did not formulate intellectual explanations of this, but he bathed us in the absurdity of our world and made us laugh, think and feel about it in his plays. Steve Allen exposes a similar world of the absurd in his thought-provoking *Whatever* by Harold Splinter, a satire on Harold Pinter.

Ionesco said that he wanted to write a tragedy but since he got into the way we have come to be, it turned out to be a comedy. Steve Allen would probably say that he wanted to write a comedy but it turned out a tragedy. As a matter of fact, Steve Allen so successfully executed his work that it turned out to be both.

Whatever forces us to encounter the meaninglessness of our daily chatter. Where are we when we need each other so badly? We are building barriers between ourselves with our small talk. It's tragic, but we have become so absurd it is funny. Allen himself has observed that we have gone from Gary Cooper to Alice Cooper. That's not only tragic—it's ridiculous. A review of our world may leave one with the impression that our history isn't just happening but is being written by someone with an absurd sense of humor such as Franz Kafka or Ionesco. Grasping the nature of this requires an extraordinary sensitivity, and in these theatre sketches Allen reveals such a sensitivity.

The juxtaposition of Hopalong Cassidy and the Jerusalem of Jesus is a creation of such grand incongruity that when I read the script to a group of students they broke out in raucous laughter. Allen has a wonderful sense of irony. In his autobiography he observes that while Christ died for love and peace Christians have turned out to be better at killing than at getting killed. What may be more absurd is that in our violent age when Christians are not involved in killing they often are simply not involved. There are no heroic Cassidys around to show care for their neighbors. There is now available a small siren one can carry around to use in the event of an attempted assault. Mort Sahl has remarked that then people will come and watch the person being assaulted. This is an absurd world, and we can get insight into the nature of it in Allen's theatre sketches.

In all of Allen's sketches big questions are raised, such as the individual versus the group or power versus morality. In *Whatever* we are shown how language can depersonalize man and make him ridiculous. In *The Westerner* it is revealed how power can demoralize and make man absurd. In *The Genius's Wife* and in *Lincoln at Home* there is an exploration of the problem of how the great man is received in life by *every man*, by the masses. The figure of the wife may be seen as symbolic of the ordinary person's incapacity to come to terms with the creative giant. If the genius is not martyred by power he may be mocked to death by the people.

WHATEVER, BY HAROLD SPLINTER

Scene: A sitting room. Everything visible is gray. A table, assorted chairs, a divan, a chest of drawers, wallpaper, doors, even the costumes of our four players—all are gray.
On the table there is a bowl of fruit. The bowl is gray. The oranges are gray. So are the bananas.
For perhaps thirty seconds no one speaks.

SARAH: (*A smartly-dressed, attractive woman, she stands looking offstage right, perhaps through a window or archway.*) Nevertheless.

IRVING: (*He is seated downstage right, looking out over the audience.*) Yes. Nevertheless indeed. And not only that but: be that as it may.

ROY: (*He is seated, center, looking straight ahead.*) You two may say what you wish but, as for me, it ill behooves me.

JENNIFER: (*She has been seated stage left but now rises, in a fury.*) I thought it would.

SARAH: Does anyone have a pencil?

IRVING: Who doesn't, in one way or another?

ROY: I have a pencil.

JENNIFER: Good for you. It will very probably stand you in good stead.

ROY: Or it will stand me in bad stead. (*Sarah moves to a bed upstage.*)

SARAH: Or I will stand on the bedstead.

JENNIFER: It's funny about beds, isn't it?

ROY: I think so.

IRVING: I don't.

JENNIFER: No, really. I mean when you get right down to it,

149

we spend a third of our life in bed. We sleep, we dream, we scratch our stomachs, we look at the ceiling and we wonder: Who's upstairs?

SARAH: But what if one lives on the top floor?

IRVING: You mean, so that there *is* no one upstairs?

SARAH: (*To audience*) That is precisely what I mean. Unless, of course, I mean something else.

ROY: I wish my mother were here.

SARAH: Do you miss her terribly?

ROY: (*Sadly*) Yes. She's gone now, God bless her. (*Looks at his watch, matter-of-factly.*) She'll be back in about twenty minutes.

JENNIFER: Is your father dead?

ROY: Yes. He died intestate.

IRVING: That must have been very painful.

JENNIFER: Irving, look me in the eye.

IRVING: I am.

JENNIFER: No. I mean the other one.

IRVING: Is there that much difference between them?

JENNFER: There must be. They don't occupy precisely the same point in space now, do they? If you don't believe it, close your right eye now and look at me with your left. Now close your left eye and look at me with the right.

IRVING: I hardly recognize you with my right eye.

ROY: (*He rises.*) Anyone for a drink? (*No answer*) Very well, then I'll have one alone. (*He pours.*)

SARAH: Oh, Roy, it's so hideous, this habitual drinking of yours. Think of it. Habitual drunkenness! And have you any excuse?

ROY: Only habitual thirst, I'm afraid. Oh, I do wish someone had a pencil. Or at least a roller skate.

SARAH: What would you *do* with a roller skate, Roy?

ROY: (*He moves to bed.*) I would put it on this bed and observe it carefully, for a very long time, I think. That's rather what life's really all about, isn't it . . . a roller skate on a bed.

SARAH: But that's absurd. You can't roller-skate on a bed.

ROY: (*Angrily*) I didn't say you could. I just said you could *put* a roller skate on a bed. I thought I made myself quite clear on that point. I said nothing whatever about skating.

SARAH: Very well. I stand corrected.

ROY: Well, you should. You're wearing orthopedic shoes.

IRVING: Can I stop looking at your left eye now?

JENNIFER: Yes, I wish you would. There's something absolutely indecent about your persistence!

ROY: (*Scathingly, in an angry outburst*) You, what would you know about persistence? I remember the night we came out of that little cafe in Monte Carlo. You had lost your last sou. But you didn't care, because no one had seen an actual sou for many years.

We were very young and very gay that night. There were stars in every swimming pool and your head was remarkably like a pumpkin (*Chuckle*) and I loved you very much as you put your hand all the way into my mouth and felt my hard palate, very carefully and deftly, like a surgeon.

IRVING: I wish you wouldn't bring up such things. You know I don't like to talk of religion.

SARAH: Oh, good God.

IRVING: There you go again. (*Pause*) It's so incredibly sad, really.

SARAH: What is?

IRVING: I'm widely experienced, world-traveled, and a thoroughly sophisticated man, but to this day I get embarrassed when a tailor measures my inseam.

JENNIFER: Why do they color alligators green, in the coloring books?

IRVING: What do you mean?

JENNIFER: When I was very young and they gave me a black-and-white drawing of an alligator to color, I always colored it green. (*Bitterly as she rises.*) What a fool I was! There are no green alligators. They're all a horrible slimy dark-gray-brown color! That's really typical of us at our best, isn't it? We get everything wrong.

151

God, what I wouldn't give right now for a good five-pound box of granulated eyelids.

SARAH: What would you do with them?

ROY: She'd probably give them all away, if I know her.

IRVING: Is that such a bad idea? That's what we ought to do with every dear thing that we own. Give it away! You know, Roy, that I do intend to mention you in my will.

ROY: How kind of you. Precisely what do you propose to bequeath to me?

IRVING: Nothing whatever.

ROY: But you just said you were going to mention me in your will.

IRVING: I did indeed. I shall, in fact, probably mention you six or seven times . . . but I shall give you nothing.

ROY: In what way then would you mention me?

IRVING: I shall point out, that you are a schmuck.

ROY: (*Looking at his watch*) Irving, I should think you'd be at the office now. Are you on hiatus?

IRVING: No, I'm on benzedrine. (*Sarah walks to a table, picks up a gray banana, peels it and takes a bite.*) May I kiss you, Sarah?

SARAH: Not while I'm eating. Anyway, if I were to grant you that privilege, you would probably spoil it. You would probably want to kiss me somewhere else than on the mouth.

ROY: You're quite right, you know. If the truth were known, I wouldn't want to kiss you on the mouth at all. As far as I'm concerned your mouth is not for kissing.

I do have considerable *interest* in your mouth, however.

SARAH: To what extent?

ROY: To the extent that I would like to punch you in it.

The only possible circumstance under which I could be induced to kiss you on the mouth was if I had injured your mouth severely and then asked you if it hurt. If you said "Yes," you might then ask me, "Would you kiss it to make it well?" Under those circumstances, and in those circumstances *only*, would I consider kissing your mouth.

SARAH: You're not making sport of me, are you?

IRVING: Sport is my dog. A dog is a very sacred thing, don't you think? I mean, a dog is more sacred than a Ping-pong ball—or a hockey puck.

JENNIFER: (*She seats herself at his side.*) Irving, you're very brave to say that. Tell me, my dear, is there anything on earth that you are really afraid of?

IRVING: I don't quite know. Sigmund Freud tells us that only two fears are natural to man, the fear of loud noises and the fear of falling.

SARAH: Do you know what Roy is afraid of, Irving?

IRVING: Yes. He's afraid of making a loud noise while falling.

JENNIFER: How very wise you are, Irving. Would you mind terribly if I killed you?

IRVING: I think not. Oh, I should mind the *pain*, of course, and I should be utterly dismayed at the sight of blood. Unless I were killed instantly. In which case I wouldn't *see* the blood, would I?

JENNIFER: No, in that case, you definitely wouldn't see the blood. Of course, anyone who *looked* at you would see it, and if those who did, later met you in the afterlife they should be able, one would think, to give you quite an accurate description of the color, the stickiness, the heat and the terrible bother of it all.

SARAH: Roy, deep down inside, are you a drinking man?

ROY: No, my dear, I never drank a man in my life. Nor do I propose to start now.
I shall never forget the first time you asked me that question. I was utterly shocked, I don't mind telling you.

JENNIFER: Do you remember what you did?

ROY: Yes, I turned on my heel. I let it run for a little while, and then I turned it off. I mean, a man can't very well travel about London with his heel running perpetually. Now, can he?

SARAH: No, I suppose he can't. You're so wise about such things.

ROY: I am indeed wise about such things, my dear. In fact, I'm wise about more than you might assume. I am, as they say, wise to *you*.

SARAH: Whatever do you mean?

IRVING: Whatever indeed. But regardless of what my mouth said, I too know what there is between you and Jennifer. I have known for quite some time now what there is between you and Jennifer.

SARAH: (*Moving toward him*) Very well. What *is* there between me and Jennifer?

IRVING: About seven and a half feet I should say. Ah, now you've stepped back a bit. Now I would say there's about eight feet between you and Jennifer.

ROY: What do you think of, dear boy, when you think of eight feet?

IRVING: I think . . . I think of the Mills Brothers. There were four of them, you know. If we consider that each of them had two feet, that adds up to eight feet.

ROY: How incredibly brilliant. But then you always were ahead of the rest of us. Somehow that really did make up for all the rest of it. It made up for all those bottles of *Scope* you kept sending us, with those childish notes signed *The Green Phantom*.

JENNIFER: (*Rising*) And will you ever forget how stunned we all were, my dear, the day the Green Phantom himself showed up? Will you ever forget how utterly dumbfounded we were to discover that the Green Phantom himself had the most utterly *un*pleasant breath that I for one have ever smelled?

ROY: Nevertheless you did go to bed with the Green Phantom, didn't you, you bitch!

JENNIFER: Of course I did. Why, should I be ashamed of it? I loved the Green Phantom very much, and that excuses a great deal, doesn't it? Yes. I loved the Green Phantom. And why not? I had always been attracted to his grandfather, the Jolly Green Giant.

I don't deny that I slept with him. I don't deny that he left me with child. Nor do I see any reason to deny that after he was killed I gave birth to a nine-pound asparagus.

SARAH: Ah, but that all happened such a very long time ago. Why do we so endlessly talk about the past?

JENNIFER: Because, you silly girl, the past is all there is.

Everything that has ever happened to us is in the past. It isn't in the future, is it?

And the present doesn't exist at all, except as a word.

ROY: Somebody gave *me* a present once of a yellow pencil. Ticonderoga.

IRVING: Was that the brand?

ROY: No, that's who gave it to me. A tall Indian chap. There was a fort named after him in an old Gary Cooper film. Fort Ticonderoga. I loved that pencil. I think I loved most of all the hard rubber eraser on the end of it. How I used to love to rub that eraser on the pathetic little papers I produced for my teachers. That was the most important thing to me in the world in those days, you know. Rubbing things out. Erasing them all. Blotting out the past, letter by letter, jot by tittle.

SARAH: Roy . . . would you be very shocked if I were to ask you to put your hand under my blouse?

ROY: Frankly, my dear, I *would* be. I would overcome my shock, you understand. I should be very honored to oblige you, in fact. But there's no question that I would be shocked.

May I put my hand under your blouse?

SARAH: Yes, you may. You'll find it in the top drawer of that dresser. It's the green blouse with white buttons. Put your hand under it and squeeze the lump of clay that you find there. Squeeze it until it oozes through your fingers. Squeeze it for dear life!

IRVING: Sarah, are those your own teeth?

SARAH: After two more payments they will be, yes. Why do you ask?

IRVING: Beats the crap out of me.

Why is one finger considered more obscene than another?

SARAH: I've heard quite enough about that subject for one night, Irving, if you don't mind. I would have told you this before now, but I haven't the slightest idea who you are. Nor have I the slightest idea what you've been talking about for the past quarter hour. Nor do I give a good goddamn, if you must know the truth.

ROY: Nor do I.

JENNIFER: Nor do I.
(*Irving looks at the audience.*)
IRVING: Altogether now.
ENTIRE AUDIENCE: Nor do I!
(*Curtain falls*)

THE WESTERNER

(The following vignette is unusual, in several ways. Because one of the characters is Christ, the reader may at first assume that the author is indulging in a Lenny Bruce exercise, but such is not the case. Allen is not being irreverent. Nor, actually, is he attempting purely to amuse, although some readers consider the following scene amusing in a way they find difficult to explain. Others may interpret it as an experiment in science fiction, or as an example of Theatre of the Absurd.)

Scene: A dusty street in ancient Jerusalem, lined with spectators, some jeering, most silent, rooted by morbid curiosity. Christ has just fallen for the third time under the crushing weight of a cumbersome wooden cross.

A sweating Roman soldier kicks angrily at the Man lying in the dust, bawls profane orders and, getting no response, removes his steaming helmet and stands for a moment wiping the perspiration from its interior. Then, methodically, he kicks again at the ribs of the silent figure lying in the street.

SOLDIER: Here, you! Get up, do you hear?
CHRIST: (*Weakly*) Yes. I—
SOLDIER: Never mind the talk, just get up! (*He begins once more to prod viciously with his toe at the prostrate body's vitals. A commotion is detected across the street and a strange figure, clad completely in black, emerges unexpectedly from the muttering rabble. The soldier stares, slack-jawed, at the newcomer's tight, black trousers and the tinkling silver objects that decorate the heels of his unusual footwear. The stranger is the first to speak.*)

156

CASSIDY: Hold on there, pardner. I wouldn't kick that hombre again if I was you!

SOLDIER: (*To Second Soldier*) What the hell do you make of this one?

SOLDIER II: Search me. They warned us about the fanatics that might try to interrupt the death march, but I—(*His hand moves toward his sheathed short sword.*)

CASSIDY: I wouldn't try anything like that either, pardner. I don't have any particular hankerin' for gun play, but you can write your own ticket.

SOLDIER: (*With remarkable patience*) Friend, we've got a job to do. I'm under orders to march this man to Calvary and unless you're carrying later instructions from Pontius Pilate you'd better stand out of the way.

SOLDIER II: That's right! There's an execution scheduled, and if you know what's good for you, you won't try to stop it!

CASSIDY: I don't reckon as how I'm aimin' to stop any execution, mister, if it's been decreed by due process of law, but there ain't any varmint so low that he deserves to be kicked when he's down.

SOLDIER: All right! Then suppose *you* get Him up on His feet.

CASSIDY: (*Squatting cowboylike in the dust*) Looks to be plumb tuckered to me. It's my guess He needs some help with this contraption.

SOLDIER: No! It doesn't do to coddle them!

SOLDIER II: That's right! He's probably faking anyway.

CASSIDY: I say this hombre needs help.

SOLDIER: (*The veins are standing out on his neck. He senses 'that he has lost face before the crowd.*) I swear if I had time I'd lock you up! All right, Mr. Know-it-all; since you're so determined the Galilean needs help to get this cross to Calvary, suppose you help Him! (*The crowd laughs. There is scattered applause, then silence as the stranger's response is awaited.*)

CASSIDY: I dealt this hand. I guess it's up to me to play it. (*He picks up the heavy wooden frame singlehandedly and a mur-*

mur goes through the crowd at the ease with which the deed is accomplished.)

SOLDIER: (*To Christ, Whose eyelids are beginning to flutter*) Come on, get up. This fellow has volunteered to help you. (*The Galilean rises and nods gratefully to Cassidy, who acknowledges the gesture with a slight smile of encouragement.*)

Together they shoulder the Cross, and the slow march resumes, inexorable as destiny.)

Exeunt Omnes

THE GENIUS'S WIFE

Scene: A more or less sixteenth-century all-purpose living room.

It may include a leaded window or two, a fireplace, bookshelves, an ancient globe, etc.

Stage left there stands an almost finished work of sculpture; nearby, on an easel, an excellent portrait, turned mostly away from the audience.

A harpsichord stands near a wall, a telescope at a window.

Downstage there is a flat-top desk or writing table, equipped with paper and quill pen.

LUDWIG VAN DA VINCI: (*A man of early middle age, clad in Renaissance attire, he sits at the harpsichord, fingering a simple phrase. Humming it to himself, he jots down a few notes on manuscript paper, then plays the phrase again this time with both hands.*) Hmmm. And so. Good. Very good.

MARTHA: (*A middle-aged servant woman, she enters, carrying a broom. After a moment she coughs softly, to attract the master's attention.*)

LUDWIG: (*He plays and hums a bit more.*)

SERVANT: Begging your pardon, sir.

LUDWIG: Eh? Oh, good morning, Martha. You startled me.

SERVANT: I'm sorry, sir. Er . . . Mrs. Van Da Vinci will be up any moment now and I was wondering if I might tidy up a bit in here before she comes down.

LUDWIG: You *don't* mean it's after nine o'clock in the morning!

SERVANT: Yes, sir. The clock you designed for the cathedral rang the hour some time ago.

LUDWIG: I've been up working since dawn. I had no *idea* what time it was.

SERVANT: Yes, sir. I was wondering if I might tidy up the floor here around the statue you've been working on. Just so the missus won't make a fuss.

LUDWIG: Of course, Martha. But mind—don't touch the *painting*. It's not quite dry yet.

SERVANT: Certainly, sir. I must say, it's the very *image* of the Crown Prince. I'm sure his majesty will be very pleased with it.

(*She begins to sweep the floor near the statue.*)

LUDWIG: Thank you, Martha. If his majesty is half as generous with his compliments about the portrait as he was toward my new symphony last week, I shall be very gratified.

Oh, I say, has old Gutenberg been here yet this morning?

SERVANT: Yes, sir. That is, he sent one of his helpers to pick up the manuscript pages you'd left. (*She chuckles.*) Though how they can make out your handwriting is more than I can understand.

But then, of course, I have enough trouble reading my own language, let alone *Latin*.

As I always say, sir, Latin is Greek to me.

LUDWIG: Is it, indeed?

SERVANT: Was it more of your poetry, sir?

LUDWIG: Was *what* . . . ?

SERVANT: The manuscript, sir. Were you writing more poetry?

LUDWIG: Oh. No, Martha. It was philosophy. I was resolving certain apparent conflicts between Aquinas and Copernicus.

SERVANT: That's nice. People shouldn't fight . . .

LUDWIG: (*Amused*) You're quite right.

ROSAMUND: (*Offstage*) Ludwig!?

LUDWIG: Yes, dear?

ROSAMUND: Are you downstairs?

LUDWIG: Yes, dear. In the study. Were there any other callers this morning, Martha?

SERVANT: Oh, yes, sir. I forgot. (*From a pocket she produces a scroll, wrapped in a red ribbon.*)

The Cardinal's man came by about an hour ago. Said to give you this letter at once. Sorry I forgot, sir.

LUDWIG: No matter. (*He takes the scroll, opens and reads it, then smiles.*)

Splendid!

SERVANT: Good news, sir?

LUDWIG: Quite! The Cardinal reports first of all that the Pope is enormously enthusiastic about my rough sketches for the new basilica—and secondly the Holy Office has ruled that my theory of planetary gravitation is not in the *least* heretical.

SERVANT: What does that *mean*, sir?

LUDWIG: It means, Martha, that you're no longer in danger of being burned at the stake for living under the same roof as a dangerous heretic.

SERVANT: Oh, thank God, sir. (*She withdraws, curtsying to the lady of the house, who enters, as if in pain.*)

LUDWIG: Good morning, my dear.

ROSAMUND: Is it? To you, perhaps.

LUDWIG: You're quite right about that. I've just gotten the most marvelous message from the Pope. He *accepts* my plans for the new basilica, and particularly compliments my design for the ceiling and roof.

ROSAMUND: (*Curtly*) Hmmm. When are you going to fix the roof of *this* house? That's what *I'd* like to know.

LUDWIG: (*He moves to harpsichord.*) I'll try to get to it today. Oh, by the way, the Duke and Duchess have invited us to the evening performance of my new concerto tomorrow night. (*She does not answer.*) You know . . . the one that goes . . . (*He plays a phrase.*)

ROSAMUND: Please! You know I can't stand that noise first thing in the morning. I really . . . (*She spies a spot on the rug.*) Oh!

LUDWIG: What's the matter?

ROSAMUND: Ruined! Ludwig, *how* many times must I tell you to put down a drop cloth when you're painting all these damned pictures! Just *look* at this spot! *Ruined!* The rug is ruined!

Mother is coming over this afternoon. She'll think we're living in a pigpen. Can't we *move* this painting out of the middle of the room? (*She does so.*)

LUDWIG: Be careful, Rosamund. Now you've smudged the paint.

ROSAMUND: Oh, who cares!? I tell you my nerves can't *stand* much more of this!

I cannot go on like this; my insomnia is getting worse all the time. I was all prepared to have a good restful sleep last night, but then you had to bring up the matter of payments on the house. And that did it. I got into bed at ten o'clock, but could I count on a good night's sleep, like other women? Oh, no. Not in *this* house. No one ever shows me any consideration around here. I'm treated just like a servant.

Just a good night's sleep—that's all I ask—but do I get any consideration? Never. So I was awake half the night. The result? Just *look* at my fingers. Look at them! Swollen to *three times* their usual size! And look at my *face*. It's the face of an old woman, the face of an old *hag*. I can't go on like this, Ludwig; I'm warning you. Things are going to have to change around here, and fast! I've had about all I can stand.

It's no wonder, after a night like that, that I can hardly *walk* this morning. My arthritis is back, and I've got the *strangest* pain in my right shoulder.

LUDWIG: Do you think perhaps . . .

ROSAMUND: No, I didn't lift anything heavy. Although, for all the help I get around here, I could lift the whole *house* and nobody would care about it. Nobody would *think* to lift a finger to help *me*.

LUDWIG: Can I . . . ?

ROSAMUND: No, I'll get my own breakfast, thank you. There've been plenty of times I *needed* help around here, but it's too late for that now. And what I'll be able to eat anyway, with the headache and upset stomach I've got, I really don't know. And why *wouldn't* I have a headache, with the lack of consideration shown me around here?

Does anybody care that my stomach cramps are back? Does anybody care that I'm a nervous *wreck*? Does anybody care that I must weigh five pounds more than I did yesterday, because of the *strain* I'm under?

No, of course not. People in this house only care about *themselves*. Well, there's a limit to everything, and there's a limit to how much I can stand. (*She moves to a side table with silver service.*)

Look at that. Did you see me almost drop that cup? I don't even have the strength in my *fingers* that I used to. And what would you *expect*, after the kind of night I've just put up with?

Look at me; my feet are so swollen I won't even be able to wear those new shoes I just bought.

Isn't that something? I *can't* . . . *even* . . . *wear* the brand-new shoes that I've been planning all *week* to wear today. But everybody *else* in this house gets all the new shoes, all the new clothes they want. They *wear* what they want when they want to, they *do* what they want, they *go* where they want; everybody looks out for himself, but not me.

Oh, no. I *never* get any consideration. I work myself to the point of exhaustion, and for what? Does anybody *appreciate* it? I tell you, things are going to have to change around here or you're all in for the shock of your lives. There's a limit to *everything*, and there's a limit to what I can take.

(*She rubs a curious finger on the telescope.*)

Look at this *dust*, will you? I told that woman to tidy up in here, but you can't trust servants any more! It's all gimme, gimme, gimme, and do as little work as possible.

LUDWIG: Yes, dear. Oh, speaking of work, you'll be glad to hear I've just completed my treatise on the metaphysical aspects of Aristotle's—

ROSAMUND: Oh, Aristotle, my ass.

Did you fix the *pump*? That's what *I'd* like to see you do—some work around this house.

Like Mr. Hildebrand across the street. Now *there's* a marvelous husband and father. He knows what's important.

LUDWIG: Yes. I ran into old Hildebrand yesterday. He was very complimentary about my B flat Minor Mass.

ROSAMUND: Yes. Your Mass. When did you last go to Mass is what *I'd* like to know. I never miss, arthritis or no, I'm down on my knees, not complaining. And God knows what I have to put up with.

You may have designed and *built* that church, Ludwig Van Da Vinci, but I *go* to it.

Yes, while you're here frittering away your time with your silly spyglass and naked statues and paintings and books. And who has to straighten *up* after you? Me! The slave. I tell you, Ludwig, I'm not going to put up with much more of the crazy goings-on in the world today—the Ren—what do you call it?

LUDWIG: The Renaissance.

ROSAMUND: Yes. Well, I've had about as much of this stupid "Renaissance" as I can take. We Europeans never appreciated the *old* days, that's *our* problem.

LUDWIG: Yes, dear.

ROSAMUND: I, for one, would like to see us go back . . . to the Dark Ages.

Curtain

ABE LINCOLN AT HOME

(*Mary Todd Lincoln is in the kitchen, keeping herself busy.*)

(*Abe enters excitedly, a sheaf of papers in his hand.*)

ABE: Honey, I've been putting a few ideas together for that speech I have to give at Gettysburg next week and I wonder if you could—

MARY: (*She starts to pour water from a pitcher into a large pan, noisily.*) Wait a minute.

ABE: Can you hear me?

MARY: What?

ABE: I want to read to you a few of these—

163

MARY: Wait a minute, Abe. You *know* I can't hear you when the water's running.

ABE: All right.

MARY: (*She stops pouring water.*) Now, what was it?

ABE: You know, I have to say a few words at Gettysburg next week and I forgot to ask my *staff* to prepare something, so I'm going to have to write it myself.

I've got a few *ideas* here that I think are sort of exciting and I'm wondering if—

MARY: (*She starts to make a great deal of noise and clatter with some pots and pans, moving them from the sink to the cupboard.*) Will you open that cupboard door for me?

ABE: (*He does so.*)

MARY: (*She puts the pots and pans into the cupboard with a great deal of noise.*) Oh, God. My back is *killing* me.

ABE: That's too bad, dear. Why don't you sit down?

MARY: Sit *down? That's* a laugh! With all I've got to do in this house? If I sit down who's going to do the *work?* Tell me *that.*

ABE: Very well. Listen, I'd like to read aloud to you just a *few* of these thoughts to see if you think they—

MARY: Oh, did you bring the *mail* in yet?

ABE: Yes, I did. I left it on the table by the door.

MARY: Good. But God knows when I'll have time to *read* it with everything I've got to do in this house. You'd think that being a President's wife I wouldn't have to lift a *finger.* Oh no. That's not the way it is, by a long shot.

ABE: Well, couldn't you just tell the servants what it is that you want—

MARY: Tell them? Abe, are you serious? I've told them a thousand times! I tell them every *morning.* But you can't get decent help any more. I talk to them till I'm blue in the face and they *still* don't know what to do. I don't know what this world is coming to.

ABE: Yes, I know what you mean. Well, listen, Mary. If I could just have your *attention* for a minute or two I'd like to just get your reaction to these few—

MARY: By the way, did you bring your soiled shirts down-stairs like I told you to?

ABE: No, I think they're still up in the closet.

MARY: Well, do you expect *me* to walk all the way up there —with my back the way it is—and do something that you could do perfectly well yourself?

You're not crippled, Abe. You can't expect me to do *everything*.

ABE: I know, Mary, but I've had quite a bit on my mind. Now listen, I was wondering if I could read a few lines of this to you, just to see how they sound.

MARY: How *what* sounds? (*She is not looking at him but continues to busy herself about the kitchen, straightening towels, inspecting for dust, etc.*)

ABE: (*Reading from a paper in his hand*) Four score and seven years ago—

MARY: Oh, my God.

ABE: What?

MARY: Do you know I *never* answered Mrs. Stanton's invitation? What will she *think* of us? Why didn't you *remind* me?

ABE: Remind you of what?

MARY: Abe Lincoln, are you listening to me? The Stantons invited us to their reception for the English ambassador and I—

ABE: Oh, I took care of that yesterday. During the cabinet meeting I told Stanton we'd be glad to come.

MARY: Well, the least you could have done is tell your own wife. How am I supposed to get things *done* around here if nobody *tells* me anything?

ABE: All right, dear. Listen, could you just give your reaction to this? Four score and seven years ago our forefathers—

MARY: (*She sits down in a chair heavily.*) My *feet* are *killing* me.

ABE: That's too bad, dear. Four score and seven years ago—

MARY: Too *bad*. Is *that* all you have to say? Well, I suppose it's these new shoes I'm wearing. I *knew* I never should have taken them but that clerk insisted they'd soften up after a few days. You can't trust sales people any more.

ABE: Four score and seven years ago our forefathers brought forth on this continent—

MARY: What *time* is it?

ABE: What?

MARY: Don't you listen to *anything?* I said "what time is it?"

ABE: It's a quarter past four. Why?

MARY: Well, I *knew* it. I knew I wouldn't have time to lie down and take a nap before dinner. I tell you, Abe. I don't know how much longer I'm going to be able to go *on* like this.

Now, what was it you wanted to tell me?

ABE: I just wanted a minute or two of your time, dear, just to get some sort of reaction to these few lines I'm considering using when I give a talk at Gettysburg next week.

MARY: Oh, and you want me to *listen,* is that it?

ABE: Yes.

MARY: Well, all right. But be quick about it, I've got a million things to do this afternoon.

ABE: (*He takes a deep breath as if to read again.*)

MARY: Oh, wait a minute. I just remembered it's time to take my *medicine.*

(*She goes to sideboard and pours herself a spoonful of medicine from a bottle.*)

Now, what were you saying about four years ago?

ABE: No, dear. I said *four score* and *seven* years ago.

MARY: Well, you mumble so. All right, go ahead.

ABE: Four score and seven years ago our forefathers . . .

MARY: You need a *haircut.*

ABE: What?

MARY: I said you need a haircut. And your *beard* needs a trimming too. Please see to it before we go to dinner at the Stantons, will you?

ABE: Yes, dear, if I can find the time.

MARY: If *you* can find the time? Now that the war's almost over what is there that keeps *you* so busy?

I just wish you'd find the time to pay a little closer attention to things in this house, Abe, that's what *I* wish. Good Lord, the place needs *painting,* the *servants* are rude; the *sink* leaks—but

166

does anybody care about such things? Oh, no. It's all left to *me*. Everything is on *my* shoulders. Well, there's a limit to my patience, Abe Lincoln. You just *remember* that.

ABE: All right, dear. Listen, I *know* you're very busy, but I'd like to get just some sort of reaction to the introduction to this—

MARY: All right, go ahead.

ABE: Eighty seven years ago—

MARY: (*Having taken a handkerchief from her pocket she blows her nose loudly, several times.*)

ABE: (*He stands waiting patiently while the noise continues.*)

MARY: God, this *cold* is driving me out of my mind. When are they going to really *heat* this barn of a place?

ABE: Perhaps if you wore that *sweater* I bought you.

MARY: What, and look like your grandmother! Why didn't you *ask* me what color I wanted?

ABE: I thought I'd surprise you.

MARY: Well, you did. And it wasn't a very *pleasant* surprise, if you must know.

ABE: (*He reads again.*) Four score and seven years ago our forefathers brought forth on this continent a new nation—

MARY: (*She starts to cough and continues to do so at considerable length and with considerable volume. After a long time she says:*) Well, go on. What are you *waiting* for?

ABE: That's all right, dear. I'll just write the rest of it on the train.

Chapter Six

POTPOURRI

In days long before Steve Allen reigned supreme as
the master of the art of talk on late night television, he was
happy just to have landed the part of a "plain-talking" cabbie
on a popular dramatic show in Hollywood. Shortly thereafter
"Scat Man" Carruthers, black musician and singer, informed
Steve that he had caught his performance on Hollywood Star
Theatre. Scat Man told Steve, "Man you really surprised me."
Allen was pleased to receive such a response to his acting ability.
At that point, however, Scat Man added, "Yes, I didn't know you
could drive a cab."

That's a funny story but Scat Man's mistake was to be surprised
at anything Steve can do. This is why it is appropriate that this
last chapter is called "Potpourri." You cannot sum up Steve Allen's talent because there are always extra odds and ends, and always an "etc." And thus in the last chapter we get odds and ends
that do not neatly fit into the other categories.

There are always odds and ends with Steve, because there are
so many Steves. His wife, Jayne, said she lives "polygamously
with eight men." Unless Steve comes home one night and catches
Jayne with one of those seven other guys, this is a great tribute.

For a big talent may be able to fool the public he entertains, but he will not be able to fool the wife he lives with. Besides, Jayne is a very gifted actress and comedienne in her own right, and thus for her to recognize how much there is to Steve is an especially important compliment.

Thus it is this gifted person we cannot really sum up whom we now try to sum up in this potpourri. It is not only funny, but you can learn from it. For example, you can learn whether or not you are a jerk since Steve has included his The National Jerk Test. In the end, however, the main test of whether you are a jerk or not may depend on whether you are open enough to laugh at life along with Steve and the great comedians.

LITTLE HIP RIDING HOOD

Once upon a time many years ago, in the land of Nod, there lived a lovely little girl named Hip Riding Hood. One day Hip Riding Hood's mother called her into the kitchen and said, "Baby, I just got word that your grandma is on a real bummer."

"What a drag," said little Hip. "What's the bit?"

"Hangoversville, for all I know," said her mother. "Anyway I've fixed up a wild basket of ribs and collard greens and I'd like you to fall by Grandma's pad this afternoon and lay the stuff on her."

"Crazy," said Hip, "and while you're at it why not add a bottle of juice? Granny would appreciate some sauce, I think."

"Mokay," said her mother.

Picking up the basket, Little Hip headed for her grandmother's cottage, going by way of the deep woods. Little did she know that a big bad wolf lurked in the heart of the forest.

She had traveled but a short distance when the wolf leaped out from behind a bush and confronted her.

"Oh," said Hip politely, "you startled me. I thought you were *Symbionese*."

"I'm on *your* side," said the wolf. "Say, you wouldn't be Little Hip Riding Hood, would you?"

"I ain't Linda Ronstadt," said Hip.

"Well, baby," said the wolf. "Gimme some skin."

"Sorry, pops," said Hip. "Some other time. Right now I have to make it over to my grandmother's place."

"Square time," said the wolf. "Why don't we have some laughs?"

"Man," said Hip, "we've had 'em. Outta my way. I gotta take a trip."

"Far out," said the wolf. "Like let's make it a twosome."

"Forget it," said Hip.

"Cool," said the wolf. "Later, baby."

So saying, the wolf bounded off through the forest and was soon lost to sight. But unbeknownst to Hip Riding Hood, he took a short cut through the trees and in a few minutes stood panting before the helpless grandmother's cottage.

Quietly he knocked at the door.

"That's a familiar beat," said Hip Riding Hood's grandmother. "Who's out there?"

"Western Union," lied the wolf. "I have a special invitation to Loggins and Messina's opening at the Bowl."

"Heavy," cried the grandmother, happily, hobbling across the room.

Imagine her horror when, upon opening the door, she perceived the wolf. In an instant he had leaped into the house, gobbled her up, and disguised himself in her night clothes.

Hearing Hip Riding Hood's footsteps on the stones of the garden path, he leaped into the poor old lady's bed and pulled the covers up over his chin.

When Hip Riding Hood knocked he said, "Hit me again. Who goes?"

"It's *me*, Gram," said Hip. "Mother heard you were feeling pretty beat. She thought you might want to pick up on some ribs."

"Nutty," said the wolf. "Fall in."

Hip Riding Hood opened the door, stepped inside, and looked around the room. "Wowie," she said. "It looks like you recorded an album here last night."

"Sorry I didn't have time to straighten up," said the wolf. "Er —what did you say was in the basket?"

"Same old jazz," said Hip.

"Baby," said the wolf, "don't put it *down*."

"I *have* to," said Hip. "It's getting *heavy*."

"I didn't come here to play straight," said the wolf. "Let's open the basket. I got eyes."

"I'm hip," said Hip. "Grandma, what groovy eyes you *have*."

"The better to *dig* you with, my dear," said the wolf.

"But, Grandma," Hip said, "I don't want to sound rude, but what a long *nose* you have."

"Yeah," said the wolf, "it's a *gasser*."

"And, Grandma," said Hip, "your *ears* are the *most*, to say the *least*."

"The better to bug your phone with, my dear," said the wolf.

"And Grandma," said Hip, "on the TV they advertise stuff that will banish unsightly facial hair. You know something? I don't want to sound like the fuzz, but you don't look like my grandmother at all."

"Baby," said the wolf, "you're freakin' out."

"No, man," insisted Hip. "I just dug your nose again and it's too much. I don't want to come right out and ask to see your ID, you understand, but where's my grandmother?"

The wolf stared at Hip Riding Hood for a long terrible moment. "Your grandmother," he said, "is *gone*."

"I'm hip," said Hip. "She swings like a pendulum do, but where *is* she?"

"She split," said the wolf.

"Don't hand me that jazz," said Hip, whereupon the wolf, being at the end of his patience, leaped out of bed and began to chase poor Hip Riding Hood about the room.

Little did he know that the wolf season had opened that very day and that a passing hunter could hear Little Hip Riding Hood's frantic cry for help.

Rushing into the cottage, the brave hunter dispatched the wolf with one bullet.

"Man," said Hip gratefully, "your timing was like the end, you know?"

And so it was.

The End

THE NATIONAL JERK TEST OR HOW TO DETERMINE IF YOU ARE A JERK

"Jerk" is a word in common usage. We frequently hear people described as jerks.

"Millie's husband is a jerk."

"Don't invite Bob to the party; he's the biggest jerk in town."

Since everyone claims to know dozens of jerks, it is reasonable to assume that jerks in our society number well into the millions.

Clearly it is past high time to do something about this alarming situation. Our society has erected machinery to deal with those who offend public sensibilities in most other ways. We are legally and technologically prepared to cope with murderers, rapists, arsonists, burglars, petty thieves, embezzlers, drug addicts, drunk drivers, etc. The task of protecting the public from such offenders is no doubt partially facilitated by the fact that *they know themselves for what they are.* A murderer, after all, is perfectly aware that he kills people. An arsonist has no doubts about the fact that he sets fire to things. The rapist well knows what his problem is. But when a *jerk* looks into a shaving mirror in the morning, apparently it never occurs to him that the face looking back is that of a jerk.

What is required, obviously, is some sort of test. After thinking of thirty or so questions for the following list I decided to accept suggestions on the open market, which revealed that there is a surprising degree of unanimity concerning jerky behavior.

As I began to collect test questions from others, however, I became aware of the necessity to weed out unusual or personal bias in the formulation of questions. For example, one man suggested that anyone who would answer "yes" to "Do you admire Vice President Agnew?" *had* to be a jerk. But a Conservative contributor suggested the question "Do you wear long hair?"

173

Obviously, such questions grow out of purely personal prejudice and are therefore not suitable for determining a degree of jerkiness that would seem reasonable to a large majority. Other rejected questions would have merely identified *ignorance*, not jerkiness. ("Can you name your senators and congressmen?") Some would have identified the quality of *squareness*. ("Do you prefer Lawrence Welk to the Beatles?")

Another category considered and rejected dealt with behavior that was simply annoying rather than jerky. ("Do you habitually forget to put the cap back on the toothpaste tube?") There's no question but that we ought all to screw the cap back on the tube when we finish with it, but neglecting to do so, however irritating to those who share the toothpaste with us, is definitely not a determinant of jerkiness.

Now, down to business:

Are you absolutely certain that you personally are not a jerk? If you have the slightest doubt, all you need do is answer the following fifty questions: *yes* or *no*.

Scoring information will be given at the conclusion of the test.

1. Have you ever written *anything* on a wall? (The wall of a men's room, a fence, a public building, etc.)

2. Have you ever thrown a roll of toilet paper at a football game?

3. Have you ever thrown garbage out of your car?

4. In a restaurant have you ever lighted a cigar and blown smoke in the faces of other diners still eating their meals?

5. When you're driving in the left lane and a motorist behind wishes to pass you on the left, as the law requires, do you ever refuse to pull over?

6. Have you ever physically threatened or attacked anyone of either sex considerably smaller than yourself?

7. Do you tell anti-Semitic, anit-Catholic, anti-Negro, or anti-Anygroup stories in mixed company *without knowing if someone present is Jewish, Catholic, Negro, or what-have-you?* (The first factor merely establishes that you are prejudiced; it's the second that marks you as a jerk.)

174

8. At a convention have you ever either (a) dropped objects out of a hotel window, (b) goosed a stranger, or (c) become belligerent as a result of drinking?

9. While seeing a play or motion picture have you ever spoken to a companion in a voice louder than a whisper?

10. In a night club have you ever actually heckled an entertainer?

11. Have you ever identified a public figure who is obviously a liberal (a Roosevelt, a Kennedy, a Humphrey, a Eugene McCarthy, a McGovern) as a Communist?

12. On an airplane, train or bus, have you ever spoken at great length to a perfect stranger in the next seat who was obviously intent upon reading a book, newspaper or magazine?

13. Have you ever—since past the age of six—written a letter to a *non*person? (A famous race horse or dog, a character on a soap opera or in a movie.)

14. Have you ever pushed anyone into a swimming pool?

15. Do you often feel a compulsion to beat other cars away from a traffic light?

16. Have you ever—since reaching the age of twelve—pasted a "Kick Me" sign on the back of an unsuspecting acquaintance?

17. Have you ever honked at the driver in front of you *within five seconds* after a traffic light turns green?

18. Do you cheer wildly when someone merely mentions your home city or state in a theater, TV or radio studio?

19. Have you ever publicly made an indecent gesture with the middle finger of your right hand?

20. Do you think motorcycles and sports cars should run with very loud, unmuffled engines?

21. Have you ever given a revolving door an extra spin, while others were still using it?

22. Have you ever—while asking a celebrity for an autograph—said, "Better be careful you're not signing any *checks* there?"

23. Have you ever asked a tall person how the weather is up there, or a short person how the weather is down there?

24. Have you ever sought free advice from a doctor or lawyer at a party?

25. Have you ever read the titles *aloud* at a silent movie?

26. Have you ever beeped your car horn going through a tunnel?

27. Have you ever revealed the surprise ending of a book, movie or play to anyone?

28. Have you ever boasted of fictitious sexual exploits?

29. Have you ever boasted of real-life sexual exploits?

30. Have you ever snapped anyone with a wet towel?

31. Have you ever written a critical letter to anyone—anonymously?

32. Do you react to criticism by attacking the person voicing it rather than by listening to the substance of what he's saying?

33. Have you ever referred to your wife as "the little woman?"

34. Did you ever say to a friend who was trying to stop drinking, "Come on, just one more little drink won't hurt?"

35. Do you put blatantly pugnacious bumper stickers (right-wing or left) on your car?

36. When you leave the table in a restaurant to go to the toilet, do you feel obliged to say: "I gotta go shake hands with my best friend," or anything else of an allegedly witty nature?

37. Do you talk a lot about your car?

38. Do you ever put catsup on a steak costing more than $6.00?

39. Have you ever had a fight with your husband (or wife) in the presence of others?

40. Have you ever spent more than thirty seconds telling someone else how drunk—or high—you had gotten on the previous evening?

41. If you are over forty-five (and neither a Negro nor a professional musician) do you frequently say things like "Like I mean, man . . ." "Right on," "Rip off," or whatever contemporary patois the young are supposed to be using?

42. Have you ever told a joke to a comedian?

43. (*For women*) Do you believe that most men *enjoy* hearing you Talk Dirty?

44. Do you say "sherbert" instead of "sherbet," or "I could care less" for "I couldn't care less?"

45. Do you touch people rather a lot when speaking to them?

46. (*For men*) Do you wear white socks with dark clothes? (In the absence of a foot infection.)

(*For women*) If you weigh over 170 pounds do you ever wear tight slacks?

47. Do you liberally sprinkle your sentences with the phrase "You know?" ("There was this guy—you know—and we saw him there—you know—and I was wonderin' what he was doin' there—you know?")

48. When you are in an audience and someone enters through the back of the room, are you unable to resist the temptation to turn and look at the newcomer?

49. Do you habitually compliment other women lavishly, in the presence of your wife? (Or other men, in the presence of your husband.)

50. Do people occasionally suggest to you that you talk too loud?

Well, there you are.

Score 2 points, of course, for each *Yes.*

If you scored somewhere *between 0 and 10*, you're a paragon of social virtue, and act jerky only on rare occasions.

Between 10 and 20: You're by no means a complete jerk, but you've got quite a few habits that definitely annoy others.

Between 20 and 30: You're a very serious offender.

Between 30 and 40: You are definitely a capital-J Jerk.

Between 40 and 50: You are one of the most irritating jerks in the annals of Jerkdom.

Anything over 50: You are hopeless. But seek help anyway. Fast.

In closing, I must thank those among my friends who provided useful test questions: Bert Prelutsky, Roger Price, Bill Harbach, Bob Bach, Portland Mason, my wife, Jayne, and my son Bill. There were two or three others who gave me good questions, too, but I seem to have forgotten their names.

(Question 51: Do you tend to forget the names of those who do favors for you?)

WHAT IS A CLYDE?

(A satire on "What Is a Boy?" "What Is a Girl?" "What Is a Husband," etc. ad infinitum)
(*To the accompaniment of emotional organ music*)

What is a Clyde?

Well, Clydes are found in the strangest places. In your crile, on the phone, from the weirdos of Greenwich Village to the Straits of Magellan, in cesspools, in filtertips, near your bird and playing on your heart strings.

A Clyde *likes*: Ferns, shtick, little black things, unmitigated gall, chicken wire, salami, Goo-Goo dolls, birdseed pudding and . . . *other* Clydes.

A Clyde *hates*: Clarinet reeds, fricassee of beaks and claws, turkey wattles, protozoa, anthracite, income taxes, or pain of headache, neuritis, neuralgia.

Nothing else can come home so frail, grove up the dell of a good bertrand so often, or lose so many file saws.

A Clyde is dignity with a stall in its fame, bronchitis with a frog in its throat, and stupidity with a bone in its mouth.

What is a Clyde made of? Well, it takes the strength of a lion, the wool of a lamb, the back of your hand, the night of the hunter, the Top of the Mark, the last of the Mohicans, and a hair of the dog.

There are several ways to *get* a Clyde. Advertise in the paper, jump in the lake, blues in the night, or punch in the mouth.

Mothers-in-law don't particularly krelm for Clydes, traffic cops grab them, little boys eat them, and Don Rickles has dinner with them.

But, you know, when you get home in the afternoon, after a long tiring day's work, when you're tired and weary and worn and sick and miserable and dirty and crummy and shaking and nervous and frightened and panicky, and drunk and raggedy and rotten and staggering and reeling and rolling in the gutter . . .

Ah, when you come home and sit down in your easy chair and that little Clyde jumps up on the bridge of your nose and sits there and stares at you, why, I tell you, friends, it just kind of makes life worthwhile to hear those three little words, "You're under arrest!"

And when the sun goes down, and the tide comes in, there is nothing finer than to breakfast in the diner. And if you can keep your Clyde, when all about you are losing theirs and blaming it on you; if you can ask yourself, "What kind of a day has it been?" then you'll know that a boom is only a ding dong, but a good cigar is a Clyde!

INCINERATORS

I rather miss the old Los Angeles incinerator. The city banned them years ago on the theory that when we got rid of the incinerators we would get rid of smog. Now the incinerators are gone, but the smog is worse than ever.

I wonder if you can remember the simple pleasure in walking out to your back yard in the evening and burning some trash. It was somehow satisfying and at least in those days you didn't have to keep trash around all week long. You could get rid of it the moment it started to accumulate.

Even Los Angeles murderers have it rougher these days now that the incinerators are gone. I remember the case of a man who killed his wife and disposed of her body by stuffing it into the incinerator. These days if you kill your wife she has to lie around all week until the trash people come by to pick her up. And if she's not in the right can, they refuse her.

One interesting thing is that a lot of the old incinerators still exist, even if they're not used. It's possible that ten thousand years from now archeologists will conclude that residents of this area had little religious shrines out in their back yards like the small shrines you see in the Orient. Obviously they were used in making burnt offerings.

EDUCATIONAL TOYS

The other day my wife brought home a toy for our baby boy. It was a small wooden mailbox with three openings in it: a square one, a round one and a triangular one. The set was completed by three wooden objects, each of which could fit only into its proper hole. The combination is described as "educational," for obvious reasons. It's brand name is *Playskool*.

A few days earlier I had bought the baby another educational toy: a tiny functional piano, the brand name of which is *Famus*.

Some day when my son is going to *skool* and has become *famus* for his daring and strangely phonetic approach to spelling, he will be thankful that we gave him only educational toys.

THE GREAT RCA-VICTOR MYSTERY

On the night of April 19, 1959, while on the air doing a commercial for RCA-Victor, it suddenly occurred to me that I had no idea who Victor was. RCA was no problem; the letters stand for Radio Corporation of America.

"But why Victor?" I ad-libbed to the twenty million people who industry statisticians assure me were watching. "RCA-*Edison* I could figure. Or RCA-*Sarnoff*. But who the heck is Victor?"

Answers were not long in coming in. They fell into two categories: those taking me to task for not knowing of the existence of the old Victor Talking Machine Company and those providing the kind of information my question was intended to unearth.

An example of the first sort came from Lawrence Laurent, television and radio editor of the Washington (D.C.) *Post*, who referred me to *Big Business and Radio* (a title which certainly puts radio in its place), written by Gleason L. Archer.

"In the spring of 1928," Mr. Laurent quoted, "conditions were peculiarly favorable for a merger of RCA and the Victor Talking Machine Company. As a result of technical developments, the radio field and the phonograph field seemed destined to coalesce into the home entertainment field. RCA could take care of this enlargement in its normal field in no better way than by an alliance with the world-famous and respected Victor Talking Machine Company. No one saw this opportunity more clearly than Owen D. Young (president of General Electric) and David Sarnoff. The Victor executives, on the other hand, now realized the necessity of acquiring rights under radio patents."

A more interesting paragraph is on pages 341 and 342. Again I quote Mr. Laurent:

"The proposed merger offered distinct possibilities. The Victor Talking Machine Company was a world-wide organization. For a generation Victor phonographs and the Victor trade-mark—the listening dog—had been known in all nations. Victor records, moreover, were being made by world-famous artists. This galaxy of talent, if brought into official relation with RCA, might supply the needs of its radio broadcasting and sound picture subsidiaries as well as insure to it a continuance of first-quality phonograph records for combination phonograph radio sets."

Since I was familiar with Victor Talking Machines and Victor Records there had never been any question in my mind as to where RCA acquired the name. Still unexplained, however, was the identity of *Victor*, assuming the word was a proper noun originally, or the reason for its use if it were a *common* noun.

Letters in the second category shed light in this area. Unfortunately they shed so much light and upon so many mutually exclusive theories that my random question promptly blossomed into a full-fledged mystery, the details of which are still a tangle of confusion.

The first clear-cut answer to the "Who was Victor?" question came from Angelo Anastasia of Monterey, California. His telegram said "After you mentioned on your program 'Who's Victor?' I called my good friend, Mr. Alexander F. Victor Master of Nipper (the Victor dog, ed.), and told him about your question. His answer: 'Who's Steve Allen?' P.S. This eighty-year-old young inventor has not been well lately so if you can, give him your good wishes."

Well, that was plain enough. But now a number of others suggested themselves. Since Alexander Victor's name was one of the best known in the world, imprinted on countless millions of records and electric appliances, why had I never heard of him? Why had the name become a household word while the man himself had faded into obscurity?

While I was pondering such questions a more puzzling element was introduced. One of the men in my office said, "We've just gotten a call from the advertising agency. They're concerned about your question about RCA-Victor."

"Why?" I said.

"I don't know," he said, "but they say the thing should be handled very carefully. They're not *complaining* that you brought it up; they don't want to make a federal case out of it, but they'd like to know the exact wording of the answer or whatever you're going to say about it next week."

"I don't know what I'm going to say yet," I said. "Tell you what. Tell the agency guys *they* can write the speech and I'll deliver it word for word."

At this point I theorized that if the top brass *had* been embarrassed by my question, it was possibly because they did not want any association made in the public's mind between the company and an aged and ill inventor who might have been nudged out of the corporate picture at sometime in the dim past. This theory, it subsequently appeared, would not hold water, but it was a reasonable first guess, given the scanty initial knowledge.

A day or two later I received a letter from a Mrs. James J. Liabocco of Woodside, California. Mrs. Liabocco's letter also gave a clear answer to my question as to the origin of the name Victor but that answer flatly contradicted the intelligence from Mr. Anastasia.

"I would like to answer your question as to what the Victor in RCA-Victor stands for," wrote Mrs. Liabocco. "My grandfather, the late Leon F. Douglas of Menlo Park, California, was the inventor of the flat-disc record. He and Mr. Eldridge Johnson founded the Victor Talking Machine Company. *This was named after my grandmother, Victoria;* (italics mine, S.A.—but you're welcome to them) the name was shortened to facilitate easier pronunciation."

So two new names had been introduced into the case; Leon Douglas and Eldridge Johnson. The next day I received a communication from none other than the son of Eldridge Johnson, *William* Johnson, who is extension librarian of the Kokomo Carnegie Library in Kokomo, Indiana. Explaining that his father was now dead and that therefore he had no way of double-checking his information, Mr. Johnson added, "It was my father's contention that the name Victor was used in the same sense that we use 'Acme' or any other term denoting excellence of the product involved."

Here then was a third theory which, like the second, came from reasonably close to the horse's mouth. It was clearly time to dispatch a note to Mr. Anastasia, my original correspondent.

"Your response to my question has us puzzled," I wrote, "in that other sources have given a different answer to the question. I would appreciate it, therefore, if you would give me more information about Mr. Alexander Victor. Did he formerly have a connection with either the RCA or the Victor companies? Were his inventions in the electrical field? What was the meaning of your identifying him as 'Master of Nipper'?"

At this point it occurred to me that I had not heard from the agency. "Call somebody over there," I instructed my secretary, "anybody. Just ask them why the name Victor is used in RCA-Victor." Several hours later she reported back.

"I've talked to three or four people there," she said. "Nobody seems to know. They've even called the factory in New Jersey and talked to the RCA-Victor people. Nobody there has any information either. The agency is going to keep checking; they'll let us know the minute they come up with anything."

"This is preposterous," I said. "One of the largest companies in the world and nobody knows where its name came from."

The following morning the agency did come up with something.

183

"As I get the story," Jules Green, our executive producer, explained, "there was a lawsuit years ago. The company won it. They came out the victor. So they decided to use the name."

"That doesn't make entire sense," I said, "unless you're leaving out important details. What did they call the company the day *before* they won the lawsuit? And what if they'd lost? Would my sponsor today be RCA-V*anquished?*"

The next piece of evidence was a telegram from Peter Bacigalupi of San Anselmo, California. "My sister Victoria," Mr. Bacigalupi explained—thus supporting Mrs. Liabocco's contention—"was married to Leon Douglas, who was the first manager of the Victor Company. Douglas named the company after his wife. He also bought the dog picture and titled it." Mr. Bacigalupi threw in the irrelevant but fascinating information that Leon Douglas had risked all the new company's capital by signing a young tenor to an exclusive contract. His name: Enrico Caruso. And Mr. Bacigalupi himself, his wire advised, had made the first movies for Edison in California.

While I was writing a note of thanks to Bacigalupi, my secretary placed on my desk a letter from another California correspondent, Alfred Wolffe of San Francisco. Mr. Wolffe's letter, interestingly enough, omitted mention of Leon Douglas altogether.

"Briefly," he wrote, "a young, far-sighted mechanic from Camden, New Jersey, named Eldridge Johnson designed and built motors for the Berliner Gramophone Company of Philadelphia. Recognizing a good thing he formed his own company: the Consolidated Talking Machine Company, which manufactured *gramophones* and gramophone records. The use of the word gramophone, however, involved him in a rather complicated court trial, from which he came out the victor. Hence the name *Victor*." This information authenticated the story we had gotten from the RCA people themselves, by way of their advertising agency, but where did it leave *Victoria* Douglas and Alexander *Victor*? Wolffe had said that Johnson worked for Berliner Gramophone Company. Who was *Berliner?*

A Mrs. Charles Vogt of Homewood, Illinois, now provided me

with a magazine clipping that further obscured matters. There was no way of determining what periodical the article had been taken from, but it was part of a larger feature that presumably explained the origin of commercial slogans or trademarks since it was headed by a picture of the Victor terrier, beneath which were the familiar words "His Master's Voice."

"Nipper," the article related, "was an alert, black-and-white fox terrier who belonged to an unknown London artist named Francis Barraud. One day Barraud wound up his studio talking machine, put on a record, and a few minutes later spotted Nipper with his head cocked, listening attentively. Barraud snatched up a brush and palette, sketched the scene, then painted it. Success came almost immediately. Public demand for copies of the painting soared. Barraud spent the rest of his life painting the scene to meet requests for it. But this was nothing. An official of the Victor Talking Machine Company bought trademark rights to the painting and promptly adopted it as the symbol of Victrola phonographs and records. . . . Today, it is the priceless possession of RCA-Victor. The name of the painting was pinned on it by Barraud and remained unchanged through the years: 'His Master's Voice.'"

The story seemed plausible, but flatly contradicted the statement Anastasia had made that Alexander Victor had been "Master of Nipper."

Right on cue Mr. Anastasia now came through with a carload of missing pieces of the puzzle. Unfortunately, after they had been fitted into place quite a few were left over. He enclosed a copy of the May 1959 issue of *The American Mercury*, which included an article by George S. Bush titled "The Great Mister Victor." Mr. Victor, it turned out, was not the castoff recluse my imagination had suggested, but a popular old millionaire in the town of Carmel, who owns a beautiful estate across from Bing Crosby's at Pebble Beach and, despite his advanced age, still putters around his laboratory, forgets to sleep, and keeps friends and neighbors amused by a constant barrage of peppery jokes.

But was he or wasn't he?

Bush states plainly: "Carmelites proudly point out the cantankerous, high-spirited little man as *the* Victor whose name adorns countless instruments and appliances of modern life. He lent his name to the Victrola and once was the real-life 'Master' of the dog in the immortal trademark 'His Master's Voice.' But mention of the phonograph annoys Victor. 'That's one thing I *didn't* invent,' he says. 'I was associated with it by accident and it never brought me anything but notoriety and trouble.'"

It is not made clear in Bush's article what Victor meant by notoriety and trouble, but on a subsequent page he gives the story of the inventor's first and presumably only connection with the record player.

"In 1898," Bush relates, "Victor, who until that time had worked only as a magician, moved into a Camden workshop to develop some illusions for his vaudeville act. The workshop was shared by Emile Berliner (him again!) and Eldridge Johnson, who were trying to perfect a new type of talking machine to take the place of Edison's cylinder apparatus.

"The big problem at the moment," says Bush, "was to prevent the gramophone needle, weighted by a heavy arm, from jumping the grooves. Victor looked over Berliner's shoulder, and said: 'My dear friend, why don't you simply build a pickup so light that the needle just barely floats over the record?' The problem was solved on the spot."

"Subsequently," according to Bush, "Johnson named the machine the *Victor Talking Machine*, perhaps in honor of the contributing magician." The word "perhaps" is tantalizing. Also significant is the fact, provided by a correspondent named Alfred Wolffe, that the Consolidated Talking Machine Company (Johnson's firm) did not adopt the name Victor until 1901, *three years after the over-the-shoulder-suggestion incident.*

"In any event," Bush continues, "he [Johnson] did not cut Victor in on the proceeds from the machine and the only thing the inventor ever got out of having his name on the phonograph was a lot of confusion. This came about when Victor went into the motion picture equipment business. . . . Now there were suddenly two prospering Victor brand names in closely allied fields that really had nothing to do with each other. This confusion has been hounding Victor ever since."

While mulling over this indeed confusing information, I received in the mail a clipping from an unidentified Monterey, California, newspaper. Part of a column called "Peninsula Parade," written by a man signing himself Professor Toro, the marked item referred to my asking the original "Who's Victor?" question and then said, "I hope that by now several thousand people have told him that this guy is Alexander Victor of Pebble Beach. As far as I know, Alexander Victor has no connection with RCA-Victor except that it got its name from the Victor Talking Machine, which is one of few things Alexander didn't invent but which was named after him because he was a friend of the people who did invent it. Got that straight, Steve?"

Not really, Professor.

Researching further I discovered that mystery-man Emile Berliner was the inventor of the flat-disc record. How this information will sit with Mrs. Liabocco, who told me that her grandfather Leon Douglas invented the flat-disc record, I do not know. But according to a publication called *Hi-Fi Guide*, Berliner turned the trick in 1888.

About 1896, Berliner, who was doing fine with his record but evidently having trouble with a machine to play it on, became associated with a mechanic, Eldridge Johnson, and the phonograph was on its way. Parenthetically Charles Edison was mistaken in his philosophy about his brain child. "I don't want the phonograph sold for amusement purposes," he said. "It is not a toy . . . no one would comprehend its value or appreciate its utility as an aid to businessmen and others for dictation purposes when seeing it only in that form."

Bush's article had cleared up very little. But what about Nipper? What did Alexander Victor have to say on this subject? As it happens, he was explicit. "Life is composed of accident," he mused for Bush. "I often took my fox terrier, Nipper, to the Camden workshop with me. One day Johnson saw Nipper with his head cocked to one side, listening to a machine. He asked the artist Francis Barraud to paint a picture of him like that. So my little Nipper became a trademark and the world's most famous dog."

If this is true, it is clearly not in agreement with the story given out to the magazine writer who elsewhere explained the origin of "His Master's Voice."

The question as to whether or not Johnson named his company after Alexander Victor may never be satisfactorily answered, but the conflicting Nipper stories seem more susceptible of authentication one way or the other since they are so extremely opposed. The one story has Nipper living in London with master Francis Barraud. Also, according to this version, the painting was a sensation long before it came to the attention of the Victor company. Art historians should know if the story is true. If it is false, what possible reason could there be for fabricating it? The first explanation which suggests itself is the "plot" theory. According to this line of thinking there would have to be a plot against Alexander Victor who, it would be feared, might seek to cut himself in on RCA-Victor profits.

On the other hand, if the Barraud story is true, what reason could Alexander Victor have for fabricating *his* version? A millionaire whose patents are numerous and whose brilliant achievements are widely respected in the communications field, he is a well-loved figure in his community, generous, intelligent, a superior individual; hardly the type to capitalize on falsehood. One possible explanation is that Alexander Victor may have become the well-intentioned victim of semantic circumstances.

Perhaps, after several years of being mistakenly identified as *the* Victor, he finally decided to float with the tide and let people think what they would without going to the trouble to personally correct every misinformed admirer. And perhaps he did own a fox terrier which used to accompany him to the Camden workshop; the dog was a popular breed at the turn of the century. It might have been a second dog that Francis Barraud painted, but the passage of time could have merged these two animals into one in Victor's memory. But all this is conjecture. Alexander Victor's story may be the true one. Unless, of course, we prefer the Victoria Douglas alternative.

After all my research I was able to go on the air and advise our viewers only that to the best of the company's knowledge the word Victor came into use because of the victory in the lawsuit of 1901.

As it stands now, nobody knows for sure. Perhaps a reader may be able to provide a final solution to the great RCA-Victor mystery.

33